D0677855

AMAZING QUESTIONS KIDS ASK ABOUT HEAVEN & ANGELS

AMAZING QUESTIONS
QUESTIONS
KIDS ASK ABOUT
Heaven & Angels

DARYL J. LUCAS, GENERAL EDITOR

DAVID R. VEERMAN, M.DIV.

JAMES C. GALVIN, ED.D.

JAMES C. WILHOIT, PH.D.

BRUCE B. BARTON, D.MIN.

RICHARD OSBORNE

Tyndale House
Publishers, Inc.
Carol Stream,
Illinois

TYNDALE is a registered trademark of Tyndale House Publishers, Inc.

Tyndale's quill logo is a trademark of Tyndale House Publishers, Inc.

Amazing Questions Kids Ask about Heaven & Angels

Copyright © 1996 by The Livingstone Corporation and Lightwave Publishing, Inc.
All rights reserved.

Illustrations by Lil Crump. "Jason and Max" © 1989 Impartation Idea, Inc.

Produced for Tyndale by Lightwave Publishing and The Livingstone Corporation.
Bruce B. Barton, James C. Galvin, David R. Veerman, Daryl J. Lucas, Livingstone
project staff.

Scripture quotations are taken from *The Simplified Living Bible,* copyright © 1990
by KNT Charitable Trust. All rights reserved. Used by permission.

ISBN-13: 978-1-4143-0800-5
ISBN-10: 1-4143-0800-0

Printed in the United States of America

10 09 08 07 06
  6   5   4   3   2   1

CONTENTS

INTRODUCTION

Children have lots of questions about heaven and angels. We know. We collected hundreds before they turned off the spigot.

Some of their questions are easy to answer, such as "Can you fall out of heaven?" But many others strike at the heart of our ignorance. Haven't you ever heard a child ask, "Why can't I see Jesus now?" Hmm . . .

Easy responses to tough questions are "I don't know," "Just because," and "Because I said so!" Those may be responses, but they're not answers. And they certainly don't help the child sort truth from error.

That's why we wrote this book: to help you answer children's tough questions about heaven and angels.

The questions come entirely from real children (with a little editing for clarity). We surveyed children ages three to twelve and collected their responses, then sorted them (the questions, not the children) until we identified the 104 most common and important ones. If you are a parent or if you work with children very often, you will surely hear questions like these—if you haven't already!

The answers, however, come entirely from Scripture. For every question, we looked in the Bible for the most relevant passages, then summarized their application to that question. Take time to study the Scriptures listed because the Bible is our final authority. God's Word alone reveals what we know about heaven and angels.

As you answer children's questions, keep the following points in mind.

- "Silly" questions are serious questions. Always take children's questions seriously. Don't laugh at them. Some questions may sound silly to you, but they're not silly to your child. Be careful not to ridicule your child's imaginative ideas.

- Some questions hide fears or insecurities. For example, when a little girl asks, "Are all people nice in heaven?" (question 42), she's asking about her own safety, not just heaven. She knows what bullies are like, and she's afraid of them. She wants assurance that in heaven no one will be mean to her or push her around. Go ahead and answer the question behind the question—assure your child that there are no bullies in heaven. If you suspect that there may be a hidden question but don't know what it is, a great way to get at it is to ask, "Why do you ask?" or "Why do you want to know?"

- The best answers come from Scripture. The Bible doesn't answer every curiosity we have, but it is our only authoritative source for information on heaven and angels. The best thing you can do to prepare to answer questions like these is to study the Scriptures yourself.

- The best answers avoid theological jargon. Use normal words. Children think in literal terms, so abstract concepts don't mean a thing to them. As much as possible, talk about *things, events,* and *objects* they can imagine. Describe a smell. Mention a thing. Talk about an action, such as running. Give them something to look at in their minds. If they can see it, they will understand it.

- Some questions have no answer. Be careful not to make up an answer when you don't have one and when the Bible is silent. If you don't have an answer, say so. Or suggest that you look for the answer together. If you get in the habit of inventing answers, your children will later lump faith with stories and superstitions they've discovered were false. Emphasize the truths of Scripture that you *do* know.

- Some kids just want to keep asking. Be ready for follow-up questions, and be willing to keep talking. Your answer may lead to more questions. That's the mark of a good answer—it makes your child think.

We wrote this book to help you answer kids' questions about heaven and angels. We sincerely hope and pray it does that.

—Dave Veerman, Jim Galvin, Jim Wilhoit, Bruce Barton,
Daryl Lucas, Rick Osborne, Lil Crump

ANGELS

Q: WHERE DID ANGELS COME FROM?

JASON'S IMAGINATION

A: God created everything, and that includes angels. The Bible doesn't say, "God created angels," nor does it mention when God created angels. But we know he did because the Bible explains that God created everything that exists. The Bible never says that God created dogs, for example, but we know that he did because he created all things. We also don't know if God created all the angels at once or if he creates them as he needs them. Angels take orders from God and serve him. They aren't equal with God and don't have the same powers as God. Remember, God didn't discover angels— he created them.

KEY VERSES: *Praise [God], all his angels, all the armies of heaven. . . . Let everything he has made give praise to him. For he gave the command, and they came into being. (Psalm 148:2, 5)*

RELATED VERSES: *Nehemiah 9:6; Colossians 1:15-16*

RELATED QUESTIONS: *On which of the seven days did God create the angels? How did God discover angels? Are angels like people except that they live in heaven? Do angels have mothers? How did God get the idea to make angels? How were angels made? Did God make angels?*

NOTE TO PARENTS: *Try to avoid using the word* angel *when it is inaccurate, such as calling your child a "little angel" or saying that a person who died has become an angel. These innocent explanations can easily confuse children.*

Q: DO ANGELS HAVE NAMES?

A: The Bible mentions two angels by name—Gabriel and Michael. We don't know if all angels have names, but they probably do since angels are personal beings, like people. Even though they don't have bodies, they have identities, just like people. But they're not human beings. They are God's servants. He created them to do his work. Remember, the only place that we can learn for sure about angels is in the Bible, God's Word.

KEY VERSE: *"Don't even ask my name," the Angel replied. "For it is a secret." (Judges 13:18)*

RELATED VERSES: *Daniel 8:16; 10:13; Luke 1:19, 26; Jude 1:9; Revelation 12:7*

RELATED QUESTIONS: *How does God remember all the angels? How come God only named two angels in the whole Bible? Was the angel's name beyond understanding because it was too hard to say (Judges 13:18)?*

Q: DO ANGELS HAVE HEARTS?

To my
Guardian angel
my very special
valentine!
xoxoxo
from Jason
+ Max

A: If you're asking whether angels have feelings, the answer is yes. Angels have feelings just as people do and just as God does. Many Bible passages tell of angels *rejoicing* whenever someone first believes in Jesus. Others tell of angels singing songs of gladness and praise to God.

Angels can also think. The Bible says they can tell the difference between good and evil. Satan and his demons used to be good angels, but they chose to do evil. (More on that in question 24.) The Bible also says that angels care about us and that they helped Jesus.

But angels don't have real hearts because they don't have physical bodies.

KEY VERSE: *There is joy among the angels of God when one sinner repents. (Luke 15:10)*

RELATED VERSES: *2 Samuel 14:17, 20; Psalm 34:7; 91:11; Luke 2:13-14; Hebrews 12:22-23; Revelation 5:11-12*

RELATED QUESTION: *Do angels get angry?*

Q: DO ANGELS GROW UP?

A: You may have seen paintings or cartoons of "baby angels," but those are not true pictures of angels. Angels don't have physical bodies, so they are never born, they never grow up, and they never die. They don't need to eat or drink, and they don't outgrow their clothes. But they can learn—they can get more knowledge than they started with. The Bible says that angels learn from watching people (they "grow in knowledge"). Angels are learning more and more of God's wisdom all the time.

KEY VERSE: *[God] wanted to show all the rulers in Heaven how perfectly wise he is. They will see the Jews and Gentiles joined together in his Church. (Ephesians 3:10)*

RELATED VERSES: *Matthew 22:30; 1 Peter 1:12*

RELATED QUESTIONS: *Do angels live like we do today? Does God have to teach his angels to do things? Do angels have ages? Can angels have children? Do angels take care of themselves? Does God tell them stories?*

NOTE TO PARENTS: *We associate growth with change. That is, we talk about people "growing" spiritually, mentally, and in other areas to describe the changes we see happening in them. When children ask, "Do angels grow up?" however, they are usually referring to physical growth—aging and getting bigger, stronger, faster, etc.*

Q: ARE ANGELS BOYS OR GIRLS?

ANGEL
IN
DISGUISE

A: *People* are either male or female (boys or girls) because of their bodies—the way they are physically. But angels don't have physical bodies, so they are neither boys nor girls. (Jesus explained that angels don't get married.) The angels Michael and Gabriel have male names, but that doesn't mean that they are men. When angels visited people in human form (when Gabriel visited Mary, for example), usually it was as a man.

KEY VERSE: *For in the resurrection there is no marriage. Everyone is like the angels in Heaven. (Matthew 22:30)*

RELATED VERSES: *Mark 12:25; 16:5; Hebrews 1:14; 13:2*

RELATED QUESTIONS: *Are there girl angels, or are they all boys? When I die, will I become an angel?*

Q: DO ANGELS GET TIRED?

A: Angels never get tired, not even a little bit, and they never sleep. They don't need sleep like you do. Good angels are incredibly powerful and always ready to do what God tells them to do. Angels can open locked doors, roll away huge stones, and even wipe out whole armies. That's because they are God's servants, and God gives them the power they need to carry out his work. Angels are not all-powerful, though. The book of Daniel tells of a time when Satan stopped an angel for a little while, until the archangel Michael came to help him. But angels never get tired, weak, or sick. And someday they will fight in the final battle against Satan and his demons—and *win*.

KEY VERSE: *Suddenly there was a great earthquake. For an Angel of the Lord came down from Heaven. He rolled aside the stone and sat on it. (Matthew 28:2)*

RELATED VERSES: *Psalm 103:20; Daniel 9:21-23; 10:13; Acts 5:19; 2 Peter 2:11; Revelation 12:7-8*

RELATED QUESTIONS: *How can angels be so strong that they were able to keep the lions' mouths from closing? Do angels help out other angels? Just how strong are angels? Do angels sleep?*

Q: DO ALL ANGELS HAVE BLONDE HAIR?

7

A: Actually, the Bible never says that angels have hair. Whenever the Bible describes them as appearing as people, it doesn't mention what color their hair is. Remember, angels don't have bodies like humans do. You may have seen paintings of angels with blonde hair, or you may have seen cartoons that show them that way, but we don't know exactly what angels looked like when they appeared to people. They *can* appear with blonde hair, but they don't have to. The Bible does say, however, that they often appeared as shining, radiant, or glorious beings. Maybe that's where people got the idea that they must have blonde hair. But then it would be just as likely that they had *red* hair. Right?

KEY VERSE: *The angels are your messengers. They are your servants of fire! (Psalm 104:4)*

RELATED VERSES: *Luke 2:9-10; John 20:12; Acts 12:7; 2 Thessalonians 1:7; Hebrews 1:7*

RELATED QUESTIONS: *What do angels look like? Are angels as bright as the sun? Are some angels black?*

Q: DO ANGELS HAVE HALOS?

8

A: Many drawings of angels or of people in the Bible show them with little rings of light over their heads that look a lot like round fluorescent light-bulbs. Those are called halos. But there is no evidence in the Bible that anyone, human or angel, ever had a halo. Real angels don't look anything like those pictures. Some passages in the Bible describe angels as very bright beings. Their clothes or their faces shine with bright light, glow like hot metal, or gleam like the sun. This is because angels reflect the glory of God. (When Moses met with God on Mount Sinai, his face took on a glow because he had been with God.) Angels don't *have* to come shining brightly, but many of them do. Halos have become a popular way of showing that angels give off God's glory or brightness, but they don't give a very good picture of the glory and power that angels actually have.

KEY VERSES: *As I [Daniel] stood there, I looked up. And suddenly there stood before me a person dressed in linen clothes. He had a belt of purest gold around his waist. And his skin was glowing and lustrous! From his face came blinding flashes like lightning. And his eyes were pools of fire. His arms and feet shone like polished brass. His voice was like the roaring of a great crowd of people. (Daniel 10:5-6)*

RELATED VERSES: *Matthew 28:2-3; Luke 2:9; 24:4; 2 Thessalonians 1:7*

RELATED QUESTIONS: *Are angels' clothes shiny? Do angels wear clothes?*

Q: WHY CAN'T I SEE ANGELS?

9

A: The Bible tells of angels appearing to people. Why don't they appear to us today? It may seem unfair or strange that you can't see angels, but angels are spirits. They don't have bodies as we do. Angels appear with physical bodies only when God sends them to speak to people. The times when angels have appeared to people (at least the ones we know about for sure) have been quite rare—only during the Exodus, the time of the judges, the time of Elijah, the time of Jesus' birth, and the time of the forming of the early church. In other words, God doesn't show off his angels. He saves angelic appearances for times when people really need to see them. Angels can do their work without being seen.

KEY VERSE: *An Angel of the Lord came and spoke to Philip. The Angel said, "Go over to the road that runs from Jerusalem through the Gaza Desert. Be there around noon." (Acts 8:26)*

RELATED VERSES: *Psalm 34:7; Acts 10:22*

RELATED QUESTIONS: *Will God let us see an angel in these days? How come God wants it so you can't see the angels? How come angels disappear?*

NOTE TO PARENTS: *The real question here may be, If angels are real, why can't I see them? Explain to your child that there are a lot of things that are real that they can't see, such as electricity, oxygen, etc.*

Q: ARE THERE PEOPLE INSIDE OF ANGELS?

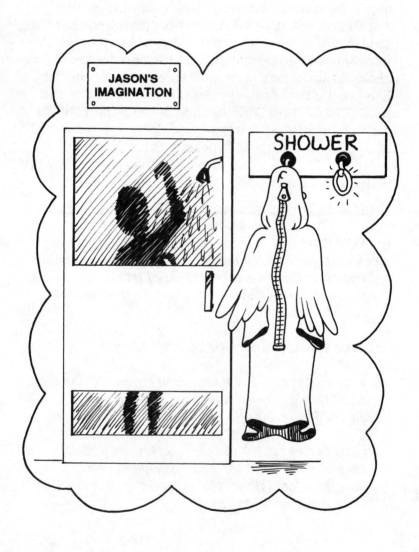

10

A: People and angels are two different kinds of beings altogether. There aren't any people inside angels, nor do people become angels when they die. In cartoons you may see people die and become angels, but that's not what really happens. People have souls. Our souls live forever as spiritual beings. In fact, here's a cool secret: When we get to heaven, we will get to rule the angels!

KEY VERSE: *Don't you know that we will judge the angels in Heaven? (1 Corinthians 6:3)*

RELATED VERSES: *Mark 12:25; Hebrews 2:5-8*

RELATED QUESTIONS: *How does a person become an angel? Were angels people before they died? Will we become angels when we get into heaven?*

Q: HOW MANY ANGELS ARE IN HEAVEN?

A: There's a huge number. We don't know how many angels are in heaven because the Bible doesn't give an exact number. But there are thousands and thousands—as many as God needs. Some people who have seen these large crowds of angels are Elisha and his servant, the shepherds at Christ's birth, and the apostle John.

KEY VERSE: *Then I [John] heard the singing of many angels. They were surrounding the throne and the Living Beings and the Elders. (Revelation 5:11)*

RELATED VERSES: *2 Kings 6:16-17; Luke 2:13; Hebrews 12:22; Revelation 7:9-11*

RELATED QUESTIONS: *How many angels are there? Does God have a sidekick angel? Does God have grandchildren in heaven?*

Q: HOW DID ANGELS GET THEIR WINGS?

A: Artists often paint angels as having wings, and people have written stories that describe angels as having wings or earning their wings. But the Bible doesn't say that all angels have wings. It does say that angels can fly and that, at times, they appear with wings. But angels don't need wings to fly, like birds or butterflies do. God made sure that they can get where they need to be when they need to be there.

KEY VERSE: *As I [Daniel] prayed, Gabriel flew swiftly to me. He is the angel I had seen in the earlier vision. (Daniel 9:21)*

RELATED VERSES: *Isaiah 6:1-2; Ezekiel 1:6-9, 23-24*

RELATED QUESTIONS: *Why do angels fly? Do angels look the same as the ones we make in the snow? Do angels really look like they do in pictures? Do all angels have wings? How come in pictures angels have wings? Do angels have wings, or do they just look like men in pajamas?*

Q: CAN ANGELS DIE?

A: If angels had bodies like people do, they would die, just like people do. But angels don't have bodies. They're spiritual beings, which means that they have no flesh or blood. Angels are spirits, invisible to us but still very real. Angels aren't born, either—they're created. Because angels don't have bodies, they can't grow old and die. But at the final judgment after the world ends, God will destroy Satan and the bad angels (see Revelation 20:11-14).

KEY VERSE: *[People] will never die again. In these ways they are like angels and are sons of God. For they are raised up in new life from the dead. (Luke 20:36)*

RELATED QUESTIONS: *If angels fight, can they get hurt? Do angels take care of themselves?*

WHAT ANGELS DO

Q: DO ANGELS GO TO WORK?

14

A: The word *angel* means "messenger." Angels don't have jobs where they work for pay, the way people do. Instead, they serve God. Angels do nothing but what God wants them to do all the time, without ever getting tired or grumpy. They're happy to do it. They do a lot of work, but they don't "go to work" like your mom or dad does.

KEY VERSE: *The angels are spirits who serve God. They are messengers sent to care for those who will receive [Christ's] salvation. (Hebrews 1:14)*

RELATED VERSES: *Luke 4:10; 16:22; Revelation 4:8; 7:15*

RELATED QUESTIONS: *What does my angel do? Can angels build things? Why does God use angels—why doesn't he do everything?*

Q: DO ANGELS WATCH TELEVISION?

15

A: Angels spend all their time doing what God wants them to do and praising him. They don't take time to relax or do things "just for fun." Keep in mind that angels don't need to relax, because they don't get tired. And they enjoy their service to God so much that stopping to do something else wouldn't be "fun" for them anyway. Why would angels want to watch the stuff on TV when they can see the stars up close, fly through the universe doing errands for God, and watch God doing miracles in people's lives? Angels have much better things to do than watch TV—they help us!

KEY VERSE: *These Living Beings . . . didn't rest day or night. They said, "Holy, holy, holy, Lord God Almighty! He was, and is, and is coming." (Revelation 4:8)*

RELATED VERSES: *Hebrews 1:14; Revelation 7:11-12*

RELATED QUESTIONS: *What do angels do all day long when they are not protecting people from getting kidnapped? Can angels get bored?*

Q: DOES EACH ANGEL BELONG TO A PERSON?

16

A: The Bible says that angels help people, but it doesn't say each angel watches over a certain person like a bodyguard. You may have heard people say that God assigns an angel to watch over each person, but we don't know whether that's true. We only know that God gives angels the job of helping and protecting us. We don't know how they divide that job.

KEY VERSE: *Be careful that you don't look down upon a single one of these children. For I [Jesus] tell you that in Heaven their angels can speak directly to my Father. (Matthew 18:10)*

RELATED VERSES: *Psalm 34:7; 91:11; Ezekiel 28:14; Hebrews 1:14*

RELATED QUESTIONS: *Does every person have a guardian angel? Do I have a guardian angel?*

NOTE TO PARENTS: *There is a Jewish tradition that angels look like the person to whom they are assigned.*

Q: ARE THERE ANGELS IN THIS ROOM WITH US?

17

A: Angels aren't everywhere, so we shouldn't expect them to be with us at every moment, the way God is. But angels *may* be in the room with you right now. Angels *can* be with us without our knowing about it. In the Bible story about Balaam (Numbers 22:21-41), Balaam didn't know there was an angel with him until God allowed him to see the angel. Angels are invisible spirits, so we never know exactly where they are.

***

KEY VERSE: *Don't forget to be kind to strangers. Some who have done this have served angels without knowing it! (Hebrews 13:2)*

RELATED VERSES: *Numbers 22:22-35; 2 Kings 6:16-17; Hebrews 1:14*

RELATED QUESTION: *Why are angels kept in heaven?*

Q: DO ANGELS STAY IN THE CAR OR FLY BESIDE?

18

A: God watches over us, using angels as his servants. If God wants an angel to be with you in the car, that is where the angel will be. If God wants the angel to be outside the car and moving along at sixty-five miles per hour, that's where the angel will be. Angels go wherever God tells them to go.

KEY VERSE: *Shall I look to the mountains for help? No! My help comes from the Lord. (Psalm 121:1-2)*

RELATED VERSE: *Matthew 28:20*

RELATED QUESTIONS: *Do angels protect us all the time? If angels are always around us, how come some people die?*

Q: DO ANGELS SIN?

19

A: We don't know if angels can sin anymore. Human beings sin because they have a desire to sin. That is because after Adam and Eve disobeyed God in the Garden of Eden, every person ever born has been born a sinner. Angels are not like human beings, and they don't have a desire to sin. So it is not natural for angels to disobey God.

The Bible hints that they may be able to do wrong. Satan was once an angel who was thrown out of heaven because he wanted to take God's place. And other angels sinned then by following Satan. But can other angels sin now? We don't know. We know only that heaven cannot have any sin in it; if it did, it would not be perfect.

KEY VERSE: *God cannot even trust his own messengers. Even angels make mistakes! (Job 4:18)*

RELATED VERSES: *Job 15:15; 2 Peter 2:4; Jude 1:6*

RELATED QUESTIONS: *Does God like it when people say to you, "Oh, you are a little angel"? Do angels do what they are supposed to do by themselves, or does God have to tell them what to do? How do angels know to obey God? If angels were bad once, can they still be bad?*

Q: CAN AN ANGEL BE YOUR FRIEND AND TELL YOU THAT HE IS YOUR ANGEL?

20

A: In the Bible, we learn that God wants to be good friends with people. He doesn't give that job to angels. God called Abraham his friend. God spoke to Moses in the way that a man would speak to a friend. That's what he wants with us, too. God's angels do his work, but they don't try to become friends with us because the one looking for our friendship is God. If God has given you an angel, you won't see that angel or talk to him.

KEY VERSE: *I [Jesus] no longer call you slaves. For a master doesn't confide in his slaves. Now you are my friends. This is proved by the fact that I have told you all that the Father told me. (John 15:15)*

RELATED VERSE: *Exodus 33:11*

RELATED QUESTIONS: *Can I talk to angels? Can you play with angels? Can you have a relationship with an angel?*

Q: DO ANGELS JUST APPEAR FOR AN INSTANT ONE MINUTE AND THEN DISAPPEAR?

21

A: Angels are not ghosts, gods, or superheroes. They serve God and always follow his directions, so they go wherever he says and appear however he tells them to. They appear to us the way they need to appear to do God's work. In the Bible we sometimes read of angels coming and going quickly, but they never did it to show off. In fact, usually no one saw them appear or disappear.

KEY VERSE: *Suddenly, the angel was joined by a great crowd of others. All the armies of Heaven were there! They were praising God. (Luke 2:13)*

RELATED VERSES: *Luke 2:8-15*

NOTE TO PARENTS: *Some children may ask this question because they think they may have seen an angel, and they want to know if it is possible. Others may ask this because of the way angels are pictured in movies and television shows. Emphasize the fact that the only reliable source for our information about angels is the Bible.*

Q: CAN AN ANGEL BE A PERSON TO US LIKE A REAL PERSON?

22

A: Sometimes angels have made themselves look like humans and have appeared to people. That's how they appeared to Abraham one day. Abraham was sitting outside his tent when three men walked up and greeted him. As far as he knew, they were men, perhaps travelers looking for a place to stay. But in fact, they were angels. That's why the Bible urges us to be kind and neighborly to visitors. You never know when a visitor might be an angel. It is possible that you have met an angel and did not know it. But don't go looking for angels. Angels almost always stay invisible.

KEY VERSE: *Don't forget to be kind to strangers. Some who have done this have served angels without knowing it! (Hebrews 13:2)*

RELATED VERSES: *Genesis 18:1-2*

RELATED QUESTIONS: *Can we talk to our angels, to the ones who protect us? Does everyone have their own personal angel?*

BAD
ANGELS

Q: ARE DEMONS RED WITH HORNS AND LONG TAILS?

23

A: Sometimes cartoons and Halloween costumes show the devil and demons as red creatures with horns and long tails. But that idea of what Satan looks like came out of someone's imagination, not from the Bible. The devil is a bad angel, and angels don't have physical bodies, so no one knows what Satan looks like. Like other angels, the devil can take different forms if he wants to. But he's not a red-clothed lizard with a pitchfork. He's a real being, living in the spiritual realm.

Satan is God's enemy, but Satan is not as powerful as God. When Satan was created, he was good. But he later rebelled against God and was kicked out of heaven. Jesus called him "a liar and the father of lies." The Bible says he is an "angel of light." So we see that Satan can be very tricky—he tries to make bad look good. His main way of doing this is to lie to us and accuse us, not scare us with the way he looks.

KEY VERSE: *I remind you of the angels who were pure and holy. But they turned to a life of sin. Now God has them chained up in prisons of darkness. They are waiting for the Judgment Day. (Jude 1:6)*

RELATED VERSE: *1 Peter 5:8*

RELATED QUESTIONS: *Who is the devil? Can demons look like angels like Satan can? Did God actually kick the devil out of heaven?*

NOTE TO PARENTS: *Kids have the idea that the devil is God's equal, like a villain in a superhero cartoon. But the devil is no match for God. God is infinite and all-powerful, while Satan is a created being with limited power.*

Q: WHY DID GOD MAKE SATAN IF GOD KNEW SATAN WOULD MAKE SIN?

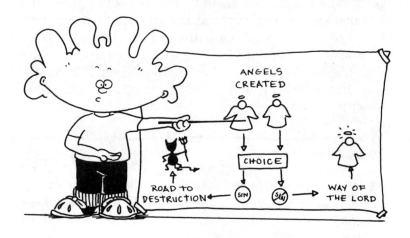

24

A: God created all people and all angels with the ability to choose to obey him. God knew that some would choose to obey and some would choose to disobey. Still he created them because he knew it was a good thing to do. God makes everything good, and that includes the people and angels, who had the choice of whether or not to serve God. Also, Satan did not invent sin, but he tries to get people to choose it. God has allowed Satan to have freedom now, but in the end God will defeat Satan and punish him.

KEY VERSE: *I [Jesus] saw Satan falling from Heaven like a flash of light! (Luke 10:18)*

RELATED VERSES: *Revelation 20:7-10*

RELATED QUESTIONS: *If heaven was so perfect and Satan lived there before he sinned, why did he sin? Why didn't God stop Adam from eating the apple off the tree? Why did God make a bad tree in the Garden with Adam and Eve?*

Q: DOES THE DEVIL HAVE POWER LIKE GOD DOES?

RUMBLE
RUMBLE

25

A: The devil has great powers, but he is not even close to being as powerful as God. Satan can perform fake miracles, lie, accuse, twist the truth, tempt, and trick people into doing what is wrong. But he also has many limits: He cannot be everywhere at the same time; he cannot create anything; he is not all-powerful; he cannot read your mind; and he has no power over Jesus.

KEY VERSES: *Dear friends, don't be afraid of those who want to murder you. They can only kill the body. They have no power over your souls. But I'll tell you whom to fear! Fear God who has the power to kill you and then put you into hell. (Luke 12:4-5)*

RELATED VERSES: *Job 1:6-12; 2:1-7; John 14:30*

RELATED QUESTIONS: *Is Satan as powerful as God? Does Satan ever get hurt? What is Satan's kingdom made up of? Why was Satan a snake when he tempted Eve?*

NOTE TO PARENTS: *You can assure your child that the devil has no power over Jesus (John 14:30). That's just one reason it's so great to be Jesus' friend.*

Q: WHAT MEAN THINGS DOES SATAN DO TO PEOPLE?

26

A: Satan does *not* get to do whatever he wants to do to people. The main thing he does is get us to hurt ourselves and others. Lots of people think that Satan only tempts people to do bad stuff. He does tempt us, but the worst thing he does is lie to us. Satan hates God and does not want us to believe what God says. He wants us to sin. He wants us to believe what is false. He wants us to believe that we are no good. Satan lies to us about our worth and about what really matters so we'll hurt ourselves. The way to see Satan's lies is to know the truth that's in the Bible, God's Word.

KEY VERSE: *Watch out for attacks from Satan, your great enemy. He prowls around like a hungry, roaring lion. He is always looking for someone to tear apart. (1 Peter 5:8)*

RELATED VERSES: *Genesis 3:1; Job 1:6-12; 2:1-7; Matthew 4:1; John 8:44; 14:30; 1 John 3:8; Revelation 12:9-10*

RELATED QUESTIONS: *Will I ever get a demon? Can people be demon possessed? Do demons live in some people's hearts?*

NOTE TO PARENTS: *Some children have heard of demon possession and wonder if it can happen to them. They may ask a question like this as a veiled way of asking the more frightening one. But the devil has no power over Jesus. If we have Jesus in our hearts, Satan won't be able to do whatever he wants to with us or make us do anything we don't want to do.*

Q: HOW COME THE DEVIL WANTS US TO BE BAD?

27

A: Satan's main purpose is to make us part of his kingdom, not just to make us bad. The devil would be quite happy if you lived a good life but never did anything for Jesus. He doesn't want you to serve God. He wants to hurt your faith in God, to make you doubt God's love and goodness. One of the ways he does that is to tempt you to do bad things. If Satan had his way, Christians would just sit around, doing nothing good and telling no one about Jesus.

KEY VERSE: *Then [false teachers] will come to their senses and escape from Satan's trap. He uses it to catch them whenever he likes. Then they can begin doing the will of God. (2 Timothy 2:26)*

RELATED VERSES: *John 17:15; 1 Peter 5:8-9*

RELATED QUESTIONS: *Why is the devil after us? Why was Satan so wicked? Why did Satan become so mean? Why is Satan so jealous? Why did Lucifer become bad?*

NOTE TO PARENTS: *Satan's main job is to lie to people, to get non-Christians to stay away from God, and to prevent Christians from serving God. He plants doubts and tries to convince us that we're not God's children.*

Q: ARE SATAN AND JESUS STILL AT WAR?

28

A: Jesus and Satan are definitely enemies at war, but Jesus will win. (By the way, when Jesus says to love your enemies, he's not talking about loving the devil. He's talking about loving people.) The devil will do everything in his power to try to stop people from believing in Jesus and living for Jesus. But we don't have to be afraid of Satan because God protects his people against Satan's power. Jesus never loses.

KEY VERSES: *Put on all of God's armor. Then you will be safe from Satan's attacks. We are not fighting against people made of flesh and blood. We are fighting against persons without bodies. They are the evil rulers of the unseen world. They are the satanic beings and evil princes of darkness who rule this world. They are the huge numbers of wicked spirits in the spirit world. (Ephesians 6:11-12)*

RELATED VERSES: *Hebrews 2:14; 1 John 2:14; Revelation 2:11; 12:7*

RELATED QUESTIONS: *Does Satan ever talk to God? Does God know the devil? Why does Satan want to be stronger than God? What does Jesus do all day? Does Jesus have a job in heaven? Does Jesus sleep?*

Q: WILL GOD FORGIVE SATAN?

29

A: God will never forgive Satan because Satan hates God and doesn't want to be forgiven. He doesn't want to have a relationship with God or to live in God's presence. He wants to take God's place. But God has already told us what will happen to Satan—he will be punished by being thrown in the lake of fire (hell), where he will suffer forever for his rebellion.

KEY VERSE: *Then the devil who tricked them will be thrown into the Lake of Fire. It is burning with sulfur where the Creature and False Prophet are. They will be tormented day and night forever and ever. (Revelation 20:10)*

RELATED VERSES: *Revelation 20:7-10*

RELATED QUESTIONS: *Can Satan turn back and become good? Why doesn't God kill Satan? If Satan knows that he isn't going to win against God, why doesn't he just become good again? Why did Satan start doing wicked things if he was an angel? Does God still love Satan, even when he does bad things to people?*

NOTE TO PARENTS: *Many people confuse niceness with God's love. They think that a loving God should be nice to everyone, even Satan. But a loving God does not love evil.*

Q: CAN AN EVIL SPIRIT STOP YOU FROM GOING TO HEAVEN?

30

A:

If a person has given his or her life to Christ, nothing can stop that person from going to heaven. The only thing the devil can do is invent lies that sound like truth and then hope people believe them. Satan can't send you to hell or keep you from going to heaven, no matter what he does.

KEY VERSES: *I am sure that nothing can ever separate us from [Christ's] love. Death can't, and life can't. The angels won't. All the powers of hell can't keep God's love away. . . . It doesn't matter if we are high above the sky, or deep in the ocean. Nothing can carry us away from God's love that is in our Lord Jesus Christ. (Romans 8:38-39)*

RELATED VERSES: *John 14:30; Philippians 1:6*

RELATED QUESTIONS: *Who goes to hell? Are there kids in hell? Can Christians go to hell? How do evil spirits come into you?*

Q: WHAT IS HELL LIKE?

31

A: According to the Bible, hell is very dark and very painful. It is a place of eternal suffering and separation from God. It is a place of grim loneliness. The worst thing about hell is that it is separate from God and from all that is good. There is no love, joy, fun, laughter, or celebration in hell. Some people make jokes about hell and say that they want to go there to be with their friends. But no one will have any friends in hell. No one should want to go there.

KEY VERSE: *But [the rich man's] soul went into hell. There, in torment, he saw Lazarus far away with Abraham. (Luke 16:23)*

RELATED VERSES: *Matthew 5:22; 8:12; 25:41, 46; 2 Thessalonians 1:9; 2 Peter 2:4; Revelation 9:1-2, 11; 14:10-11; 20:10*

RELATED QUESTIONS: *Why is there hell? Where is hell? Is there fire in hell? Why is hell dark if they have fires? Is it hot in hell? Was there a fire when the devil went down to hell?*

NOTE TO PARENTS: *Be very serious when you explain hell to your children. At the same time, however, tell them about heaven, a place of eternal love, joy, fun, laughter, and celebration. And assure them that they can go to heaven if they trust in Jesus.*

ANGELS
IN THE
BIBLE

Q: WHY DID AN ANGEL COME TO MARY?

32

A: An angel came to Mary to tell her God's message—God wanted Mary to know that she would be the mother of Jesus, God's Son. When Mary heard the news, she was frightened, but she was also very happy. More than anything, she wanted to obey God. And she felt very honored to be Jesus' mother.

KEY VERSE: *God sent the angel Gabriel to Nazareth. (Luke 1:26)*

RELATED VERSES: *Luke 1:26-38*

RELATED QUESTIONS: *What was the name of the angel who came to Mary? What angel came to tell the shepherds about Jesus' birth?*

NOTE TO PARENTS: *This is a good time to let your children know that God is able to show them his plan for their lives. God's plan probably won't be announced by an angel, but God will tell it to them when they seek him.*

Q: WHY WAS THERE AN ANGEL AND A FIERY SWORD GUARDING THE ENTRANCE TO THE GARDEN OF EDEN?

33

A: An angel stood at the entrance to the Garden of Eden to keep Adam and Eve from going back in. God had sent them out of the Garden because they had sinned. Because they disobeyed God, they would never be allowed to live in Eden again.

KEY VERSE: *God expelled [Adam]. And God placed mighty angels at the east of the Garden of Eden. They stood with a flaming sword to guard the entrance to the Tree of Life. (Genesis 3:24)*

RELATED VERSES: *Numbers 22:31; 1 Chronicles 21:27-30; Luke 4:10*

RELATED QUESTIONS: *How did Satan disguise himself as a snake? Did the serpent bite? When you're in heaven, can you still see the angel that is guarding the entrance to Eden? Did Adam and Eve go to heaven when they died?*

Q: WHO WAS THE ANGEL OF THE LORD?

34

A: The Bible mentions the angel of the Lord many times. In the desert, when Moses saw the bush that was burning but wasn't burning up, it was the angel of the Lord who spoke to him out of it. Who was this who spoke? Some people think it was a special appearance of God and not actually an angel. But usually the phrase "angel of the Lord" is just a good way to describe an angel. It probably does not refer to one specific angel.

KEY VERSE: *The Angel of the Lord came to [Gideon]. He said, "Mighty soldier, the Lord is with you!" (Judges 6:12)*

RELATED VERSES: *Exodus 3:2; Numbers 22:22; 2 Samuel 24:16; 1 Chronicles 21:16*

RELATED QUESTION: *Why do people call an angel "angel of the Lord"?*

NOTE TO PARENTS: *It is important to help your child focus on God, not on angels. The message sender and the message are most important, not the messengers.*

Q: WHY DO SOME ANGELS LOOK LIKE REAL PEOPLE?

35

A: The word *angel* means "messenger," and God sometimes sends these messengers to take messages to people. The Bible describes them as bringing these messages while in the form of human beings. God can send angels to encourage a person, comfort someone, or merely to deliver news. If angels always appeared as blazing towers of fire, they would scare people away. Sometimes God wants angels to frighten people. But at other times he wants his messengers to hide their true identity as angels for a while; then they appear as people.

KEY VERSE: *All at once [Abraham] saw three men coming toward him. He jumped up and ran to meet them and welcomed them. (Genesis 18:2)*

RELATED VERSES: *Genesis 19:1; Judges 6:11-12; 13:15-18; Daniel 9:21; Acts 12:7; Hebrews 1:14*

RELATED QUESTION: *Can angels be here with us?*

Q: WHY DO SOME ANGELS HAVE FOUR FACES?

36

A: When the Bible describes angels as having four faces, it is not giving us a picture of what angels actually look like (like a photograph). Remember, angels don't have physical bodies, so they don't have faces the way people do. When a prophet saw an angel with four faces, God was telling him that angels have many abilities—that angels show us several things about God, that they can see in any direction, and that they can serve God in any way needed at any time.

KEY VERSE: *Each of the four Guardian Angels had four faces. The first was that of an ox. The second was a man's face. The third was a lion's face. And the fourth was an eagle's face. (Ezekiel 10:14)*

RELATED VERSES: *Ezekiel 10:1-22*

Q: WHY DIDN'T AN ANGEL TAKE JESUS OFF THE CROSS?

37

A: It was God's will for Jesus to die on the cross. Jesus could have called on thousands of angels to rescue him, but he did not do that because he was dying for us, taking the punishment for our sins. If angels had stepped in and rescued Jesus, he would not have died, and then we would not be forgiven. Jesus' disciple Peter tried to stop Jesus from being arrested, but Jesus told him not to do that because it was God's plan for him to die.

Just before Jesus died, he cried out, "My God, my God, why have you forsaken me?" meaning that God had left him totally alone. No one was there to help him or comfort him, not even the angels. This was part of his suffering for our sins.

KEY VERSES: *Don't you know that I [Jesus] could call on my Father? He could send thousands of angels to keep us safe! And he could send them right away! But if I did this, how would the Scriptures be fulfilled? For they foretold what is happening now. (Matthew 26:53-54)*

RELATED VERSES: *Matthew 26:51-54; Mark 8:31; 15:34-37*

RELATED QUESTIONS: *Where were the angels when Jesus died? Why didn't an angel take Jesus' crown off of him? Why did an angel come to the tomb after Jesus had left?*

38

A: The Bible uses the word *archangel* to describe one type of angel that seems to be more important than regular angels. Only Michael is said to be an archangel, but we don't know if he is the only one. The Bible also refers to princes among the angels. That seems to suggest that some angels are more powerful than others. Angels are not equal to Jesus, though. They aren't gods, nor are they God's buddies. Angels are created beings who obey and worship God.

KEY VERSE: *For 21 days the Evil Spirit who rules the kingdom of Persia blocked my [the angel's] way. Then Michael, one of the top officers of the heavenly army, came to help me. So I was able to get past these spirit rulers of Persia. (Daniel 10:13)*

RELATED VERSES: *Daniel 10:21; 1 Thessalonians 4:16; Hebrews 1:3-13; 2:5-8; Jude 1:9*

RELATED QUESTION: *Does God have a bodyguard?*

Q: WHY ARE SOME PEOPLE SCARED OF ANGELS?

39

A: In the Bible, we read that some people became frightened when angels appeared to them. They were scared because they were amazed at the power and glory of the angels. God is great and holy and awesome, and sometimes angels appear with a lot of light and noise. That can be quite scary. Also, remember that most people have never seen an angel. So when one appears, it is quite normal to be surprised and fearful. Many times when angels appeared, they had to tell the people they visited not to be afraid. God sends angels to us to help us, so we don't need to be afraid of them.

KEY VERSE: *Then the Angel touched the meat and bread with his staff. Fire flamed up from the rock and burned them up! And suddenly the Angel was gone! (Judges 6:21)*

RELATED VERSES: *1 Chronicles 21:30; Matthew 28:2-4; Luke 1:13, 28-30; 2:9-10; Revelation 22:8-9*

HEAVEN

Q: WHY DID GOD MAKE HEAVEN?

40

A: God has only one use for heaven, and that is to share it with us. God is everywhere. When we talk about heaven, we are really talking about where God lives. We think of heaven as a place because that's how we describe going to be with God. But remember, God isn't just in one place—he's everywhere!

In the Bible, the word *heaven* can refer to several places: (1) the home or place of God; (2) the new Jerusalem; or (3) "the heavens," or sky. Just before Jesus left the earth, he said he would go and prepare a place for us, a place where we can live with him. Someday he will come back and set it all up for us—he will destroy this world and create a new one. That new world will be for all those who love him. That's the heaven that God will make for all believers to live in forever.

KEY VERSES: *There are many homes in my Father's house. I am going to prepare a place for you. I will come again and take you to me. Then you will be with me where I am about to go. If this weren't so, I would tell you plainly. (John 14:2-3)*

RELATED VERSES: *Hebrews 9:24; Revelation 21:3*

RELATED QUESTIONS: *What is heaven? What is heaven like? Why did God come to the earth? Is hell near heaven?*

NOTE TO PARENTS: *Heaven is one of the Christian's great hopes. It is God's guarantee that the evil, injustice, and cruelty of life here on earth will end and be put right. People without hope in Christ can feel overwhelmed by fear of the future, but Christians need not be afraid. Share this hope with your child.*

Q: IS JESUS THE ONLY WAY TO HEAVEN?

41

A: Yes, Jesus is the only way to heaven. He said, "No one can get to the Father except through me." Just as the only right answer to 2 + 2 is 4, Jesus is the only answer to our need for forgiveness. He is the only one who has the right to take away our sins, since he died for us. He is the only one who has the power to take them away, since he is God. And he is the only one who can be perfectly fair to every single person, from babies never born to the most wicked person who ever lived, since he is just and merciful. Since Jesus has offered a clear way to heaven, why would anyone look for any other way?

KEY VERSE: *Jesus said, "I am the Way, the Truth, and the Life. No one can get to the Father except through me." (John 14:6)*

RELATED VERSES: *John 6:68; Revelation 22:17*

RELATED QUESTIONS: *Why is heaven the only way? If you believe in God but you never asked Jesus as your Lord and Savior, can you still go to heaven? If babies die before they are born, do they go to heaven?*

NOTE TO PARENTS: *A question like this usually means that other children were discussing their beliefs with your child. Take this time to reassure your child that belief in Christ is the only way to heaven, and take some time to pray with your child for his or her friends.*

Q: ARE ALL PEOPLE NICE IN HEAVEN?

42

A: All the people in heaven are nice because everyone there loves God and loves one another. No one will hurt anyone or be mean to anyone in heaven. There will be no crying or pain. There will be no pushing or shoving or name-calling in heaven. The Bible says that in heaven we will know God like he knows us. When we know and understand God and his love, we won't want to hurt anyone ever again.

KEY VERSE: *Don't you know that those doing such [evil] things can't share in God's Kingdom? (1 Corinthians 6:9)*

RELATED VERSES: *Revelation 21:4, 8; 22:14-15*

RELATED QUESTIONS: *Will bullies call me names in heaven? What if someone bad tricks Jesus and sneaks into heaven and hits people?*

NOTE TO PARENTS: *Be careful not to give the impression that being nice gets you into heaven. While all people of God should be kind, not all kind people are people of God. Also, the question behind the question here may involve fear of others—the child wants assurance that in heaven no one will hurt him or her. You can assure your child that there are no bullies in heaven. Heaven is the safest, most wonderful place ever made.*

Q: CAN YOU FALL OUT OF HEAVEN?

43

A: People cannot fall out of heaven any more than they can fall out of their own front yard. You may have seen pictures or cartoons that show heaven as a place up in the sky or in the clouds. We don't know where heaven is; we only know that God and Jesus are there. Someday God will make a new earth and a new city called the new Jerusalem, where all his people will live forever. That place will be perfect for us—no dangerous streets, no diseases to catch, nothing to worry about at all. In heaven, you will never hear anyone say, "Be careful!" because you won't have any dangers to be careful about.

KEY VERSE: *I heard a loud shout from the throne. It was saying, "Look, the home of God is now among men. He will live with them and they will be his people. Yes, God himself will be among them." (Revelation 21:3)*

RELATED VERSES: *Romans 8:39; Revelation 22:14*

RELATED QUESTIONS: *Are there police in heaven? Will there be any doors in heaven? Does heaven move?*

NOTE TO PARENTS: *This question comes up when children confuse heaven with a physical location, usually one that is up in the sky. They are not able to imagine a spiritual—as opposed to physical—reality, so they can't imagine heaven not being a place. They naturally think of heaven as being up because that's where we put it in our descriptions of it.*

HEAVEN

Q: IS HEAVEN ALL MADE UP OF CLOUDS?

44

A: Sometimes cartoons and movies show funny pictures of angels standing in clouds. But heaven is not made up of clouds. The Bible does say that clouds surround God's throne, that Jesus was caught up in the clouds, and that when Jesus returns he will come in the clouds. But those are word pictures. They don't mean that heaven is made up of rain clouds. Heaven is God's presence. It's a spiritual place. It's a world invisible to us now but very real just the same.

KEY VERSE: *Then the scene changed. I saw a white cloud. Someone was sitting on it, and he looked like Jesus. He was called "The Son of Man." He had a crown of gold on his head and a sickle in his hand. (Revelation 14:14)*

RELATED VERSES: *Psalm 97:2; Luke 21:27; 1 Thessalonians 4:17*

RELATED QUESTIONS: *Is there going to be summer and fall in heaven? Will there be any winter? Will our house be warm? Does it rain in heaven? Can you walk on clouds in heaven? Are there bathrooms in heaven? Is there water in heaven?*

NOTE TO PARENTS: *Children pick up a lot of wrong ideas about heaven from cartoons and other popular tales. If you're not sure how to explain what's wrong with a false idea, it's better to say "I don't know how to explain it" than to fall back on a popular fantasy. Sit down with them and read Revelation 21–22 together so they can see what the Bible says about heaven and the new Jerusalem.*

Q: WHY IS HEAVEN SO SHINY?

45

A: Heaven shines with the brightness of the glory of God. God is perfect, holy, 100 percent good. Because of that, God shines with light. Many descriptions of heaven mention light and gold because of God's glory.

KEY VERSE: *Great bursts of light flashed forth from him. It was like light from a glittering diamond or from a shining ruby. There was a rainbow glowing like an emerald around his throne. (Revelation 4:3)*

RELATED VERSES: *Revelation 4:1-6; 21:18-21, 23; 22:5*

RELATED QUESTIONS: *Will there be night in heaven? Why does God stay up all night? What does my mansion in heaven look like?*

Q: ARE THE STREETS IN HEAVEN REAL GOLD OR JUST PAINTED WITH GOLD?

46

A: All of heaven is real—none of it is fake. When we get there, it will be the most real, beautiful place we have ever seen. Will even the gold be real? The Bible says that the streets will be paved with gold. This may just be a way of saying that it's a great place to be, like saying "It must be a million degrees out here" to describe a really hot day. Or it may refer to real gold streets running through town. It's hard to know *exactly* what heaven will be like because we really can't understand it now.

Imagine a frog trying to explain life on land to a tadpole. All the descriptions would sound bad—you can't swim, there's no water, etc. The frog can't really tell the tadpole what life on land is like. Only when the tadpole becomes a frog can the tadpole understand. Only when we get to heaven will we know what it will be like. But one thing is for sure: Nothing will be fake!

KEY VERSE: *The 12 gates were made of pearls. Each gate was made from a single pearl! And the main street was pure, clear gold, like glass. (Revelation 21:21)*

RELATED VERSES: *Revelation 21:1–22:21*

RELATED QUESTIONS: *What will God's house be made of? What will God's house look like in heaven? Is heaven more beautiful than the most beautiful place on earth? What is heaven made of? How does God make things out of gold? Does God use glue to make gold stick to the new Jerusalem? Are the gates in heaven made out of gold?*

Q: DOES GOD HAVE ANGELS WATCHING OVER HEAVEN SO DEMONS CAN'T GET IN?

47

A: God will let no evil at all into heaven—no sin, no hurting, no demons. Life in heaven will be *safe*. In fact, heaven is the safest place anywhere—perfectly safe all the time. No one in heaven is afraid of anything, and no one there ever gets hurt.

KEY VERSE: *[God] will swallow up death forever. The Lord God will wipe away all tears. He will take away all insults and mockery against his land and people forever. The Lord has spoken! He will surely do it! (Isaiah 25:8)*

RELATED VERSES: *Revelation 7:17; 22:3-5*

RELATED QUESTIONS: *Is heaven a safe place? Will I be safe in heaven? Does God keep bad stuff out of heaven? Can the devil still hurt you when you're in heaven? Will snakes be there? Will we be able to see Satan in heaven?*

NOTE TO PARENTS: *Every child craves safety and fears danger. A safe place is a happy place, and conversely, a dangerous place isn't. In order to be happy, a child needs to feel safe. A question like this one, therefore, applies a child's test of happiness to heaven: If it isn't safe, then it can't be happy. You can reassure your child that no place is safer than heaven.*

Q: WHERE DID GOD LIVE BEFORE HEAVEN WAS MADE?

48

A: God has always lived in heaven because heaven is the place where God is. God has made a place for us where he is—so that is heaven for us. Wherever God is, there is heaven.

KEY VERSE: *Our Father in Heaven, we honor your holy name. (Matthew 6:9)*

RELATED VERSES: *Deuteronomy 26:15; 1 Kings 8:30, 39, 43, 49*

RELATED QUESTIONS: *Where does God live? How does God get down here (to live in us)—does he fly? How can God be in more than one place at one time? How long did it take to make heaven?*

NOTE TO PARENTS: *Sometimes a child's question comes from a faulty assumption about God. You can use questions like this to explain how God is different from us.*

49

A: When Jesus left the earth, he went to heaven to live with God the Father. That's where he is right now. He sits at the Father's right hand, the place of highest honor. The Bible says he talks to God about us (1 John 2:1).

KEY VERSE: *Now I am leaving the world, and leaving them behind. And I am coming to you. Holy Father, keep them in your own care. Keep all those you have given me. May they be united just as we are. (John 17:11)*

RELATED VERSES: *John 17:5; Acts 7:55-56; Romans 8:34; Colossians 3:1; Hebrews 10:12*

RELATED QUESTIONS: *Will Jesus do miracles in heaven? Is Jesus happy in heaven? When God is in heaven, is he always thinking of people down here on earth? Does God take care of his angels the way he takes care of his people? Is God like the president of the United States in heaven?*

Q: WHY DOESN'T GOD TAKE US TO HEAVEN AS SOON AS WE GET SAVED?

50

A: God doesn't take his people to heaven right away because he wants them to grow in their faith. He also wants them to tell others about Christ, to help others, and to make the world better. God has work for his people to do.

KEY VERSES: *So now go and make disciples in all the nations. Baptize them into the name of the Father, the Son, and the Holy Spirit. Then teach these new disciples to obey all the commands I have given you. (Matthew 28:19-20)*

RELATED VERSES: *John 9:4; 2 Peter 3:9*

Q: WHAT IF I DON'T WANT TO LEAVE MY FRIENDS AND FAMILY TO GO TO HEAVEN?

51

A: It's OK to not want to go to heaven right now. God has given you a place to enjoy right here and now—your home and your family and friends. You don't have to go to heaven right away.

But heaven will be a happy place, not a lonely or a sad place. Once you're in heaven you won't feel afraid of it—you will be glad that you are there. And if your family and friends know Jesus, too, you all will be in heaven together. You will be together with your family again.

KEY VERSE: *Be sure of this thing! I am with you always, even to the end of the world. (Matthew 28:20)*

RELATED VERSES: *Revelation 21:3-5*

RELATED QUESTIONS: *Will I be able to play with my friends up in heaven? How can you get out of heaven? What will my friend do when he goes to heaven? Do they have sports in heaven?*

NOTE TO PARENTS: *Don't be appalled if your child says he or she is afraid of heaven or doesn't want to go. Some kids fear going to heaven because it seems faraway and mysterious. All they can imagine is being taken away from their families and going to a cold and impersonal place where they don't know anyone. Assure your child that heaven is a warm and happy place.*

Q: HOW LONG DOES IT TAKE TO GET TO HEAVEN FROM HERE?

52

A: It happens in an instant. It's like opening your eyes—you're suddenly there. That's because heaven isn't a faraway place but is the place where God is. He just takes you there. The Bible says that when Jesus comes back, he will change us "in the twinkling of an eye."

KEY VERSE: *It will all happen in a moment, in the twinkling of an eye. (1 Corinthians 15:52)*

RELATED VERSES: *2 Corinthians 5:6-8; Philippians 1:21-23; 1 Thessalonians 4:13-17*

RELATED QUESTIONS: *Is heaven far out in space? Where is heaven? Can birds just fly into heaven anytime they want to? If we went high enough into the sky, would we find heaven? Why can't we go to heaven and just see it and then come back? When you die, are you just dead for a few seconds and then you're in heaven?*

Q: DOES GOD PUT DOWN A LADDER TO BRING US TO HEAVEN?

53

A: God takes us to heaven as soon as we die—immediately. God doesn't need a ladder or an airplane or anything else; we will just be there with him. The Bible says that Jesus is preparing a place for us. Through faith in him, we can have forgiveness of sins. Then, when it comes time for God to take us to heaven, he will do it—he will take us to live with him in his home forever.

KEY VERSE: *The Lord himself will come down from Heaven. This will happen with a mighty shout. There will be the voice of the archangel and a trumpet of God. The believers who are dead will be the first to rise to meet the Lord. (1 Thessalonians 4:16)*

RELATED VERSES: *Luke 16:22-31; John 14:6*

RELATED QUESTIONS: *Do angels take people's souls up to heaven? Will Jesus help me fly up? How will Jesus get me there? How do we get to heaven? How does God get people to heaven? Does God put down a ladder so that when people die they just climb up it into heaven? Do angels carry me to heaven? Does God take us to heaven? Does Jesus come for you with his body?*

NOTE TO PARENTS: *This question can mean two things: (1) What method does God use to transport us to heaven? and (2) How can a person be forgiven and go to heaven? Make sure you know which question your child means. In Jesus' story about the rich man and Lazarus (Luke 16:22), he mentioned that the angels carried Lazarus to heaven. Angels may be involved in the process.*

WHEN PEOPLE DIE

Q: WHY DO PEOPLE DIE?

54

A: People die because of sin. When God created the first human beings, they weren't supposed to die. They would never grow old or wear out. But then they disobeyed God, and sin and death entered the world. From that point on, every person born has been born a sinner into a sinful world. With sin came death, and so plants, animals, and people started to die. *Every* person has to die. But people can live eternally, in heaven with God, if they trust in Christ and ask God to forgive their sins. In heaven we aren't broken anymore. There is no sickness or pain or dying there.

KEY VERSES: *You may eat any fruit in the garden except fruit from the Tree of Conscience. You must not eat from that tree. For its fruit will open your eyes. It will make you aware of right and wrong, good and bad. If you eat its fruit, you will be doomed to die. (Genesis 2:16-17)*

RELATED VERSES: *Romans 6:23; 1 Corinthians 15:22; Hebrews 9:27; James 1:15*

RELATED QUESTIONS: *What is death? Why do I have to die? Why do some people die when they're young and not just when they're old? If God wants everyone to live, why do babies die? Do you grow older when you go to heaven?*

NOTE TO PARENTS: *This question often comes up when a relative or a pet dies. It is a good question and an important one for you to answer because it creates a "teachable moment." Answering it will probably lead to several more questions about salvation, eternal life, and heaven, so be prepared!*

Q: DOES YOUR BODY STAY IN THE GRAVE WHEN YOU GO TO HEAVEN?

55

A: The body you have here on earth is a physical, imperfect, short-term holding place for your soul. It's not made to last. When it's dead, it will decay. The real you is your soul, not your body. But in heaven you will be given a new body, a body that will last forever. This is known as the resurrection. The physical body will die, but the spiritual body will last forever. What happens to your body on earth or in the grave will not affect your eternal life in any way.

KEY VERSE: *For you [God] will not leave me among the dead. You will not let your loved one rot in the grave. (Psalm 16:10)*

RELATED VERSES: *Psalm 49:15; 1 Corinthians 15:35, 42-44*

RELATED QUESTIONS: *Will we be able to breathe in heaven? Does your spirit have clothes on when it leaves your body, or is it naked? What does it feel like when your spirit leaves your body? When you die are you automatically in heaven?*

Q: WILL I GO TO HEAVEN WHEN I DIE?

56

A: Every person who trusts in Jesus gets to go to heaven. If you have asked Jesus to take away your sins, then you will go to heaven, too. That's God's promise. And nothing can take away God's promise of heaven. When you die as a Christian, you go straight to live with God—you don't need to be afraid of dying.

KEY VERSE: *It is God's will that I should not lose even one of all those he has given me. It is his will that I should raise them to eternal life at the Last Day. (John 6:39)*

RELATED VERSES: *Isaiah 12:2; Romans 8:38-39; Hebrews 2:14; 6:11; 10:19-22; 2 Peter 1:10-11; 1 John 5:13*

RELATED QUESTIONS: *What if I die when I'm six or seven or eight? When will I die? When will we be dead? When I die, will I go straight to heaven?*

NOTE TO PARENTS: *Many children have a profound fear of death. They may have nightmares about it. But they may also hesitate to talk about it with you, so you may not hear them ask about it. Reassure them: Jesus defeated death. He made it possible for us to live forever in heaven. We don't need to fear death.*

Q: IS THERE ANY OTHER PLACE YOU CAN GO TO BESIDES HEAVEN OR HELL WHEN YOU DIE?

57

A: You may have heard people talk about purgatory, limbo, or some other in-between place where people go after they die. But the Bible does not teach anything about a place like that. The Bible does teach, however, that death is the final cutoff point. People do not have a second chance after they die. There is no opportunity after death to undo the bad things a person did while alive. The Bible also makes it very clear that Christians immediately go to be with God after they die.

KEY VERSE: *Jesus replied, "Today you will be with me in Paradise. This is a solemn promise." (Luke 23:43)*

RELATED VERSES: *Psalm 86:13; Proverbs 1:12; Luke 23:40-43; Hebrews 9:27*

RELATED QUESTION: *Does your soul stay in your body until you are buried or just until you die?*

Q: CAN GOD TAKE YOU TO HEAVEN IF YOU'RE NOT DEAD YET?

58

A: God can do anything. He can take a person to heaven anytime he likes, even if that person has not died. And in fact, the Bible tells about two people who had that privilege: Enoch and Elijah. God took them directly to heaven before they died. The Bible also tells us that someday Jesus will come back and take all his people to heaven, even those who have not died yet.

KEY VERSE: *When [Enoch] was 365, he disappeared. God took him away! (Genesis 5:24)*

RELATED VERSES: *2 Kings 2:11-12; 1 Corinthians 15:51; 1 Thessalonians 4:15-17*

RELATED QUESTIONS: *Why did Elijah get taken into heaven by a whirlwind when he hadn't died yet? Will we go to heaven in a fiery chariot?*

Q: WHY ARE CEMETERIES SO CREEPY?

59

A: Death is a scary thing because it is final. After a person dies, that person does not come back to earth ever again. It's not like going on a trip and then coming back. It's like going on a trip and *never* coming back.

Death also scares us because it can happen so suddenly. One second the person is here, awake and talking. Then he or she is dead, unable to talk or live with us ever again.

That's why cemeteries are so creepy. No one wants to die, and cemeteries are where dead bodies are buried. Also, television and movies show cemeteries as places where ghosts and other spooky things hang out. Because most people fear death, a cemetery can be a scary place. But Christians don't have to be afraid of death because they know that they will go to heaven when they die and that scary things are just made up by people who make movies and TV shows.

KEY VERSES: *Even now, just as in the past, I hope that I will be an honor to Christ. This is true whether I live or die. For to me, living is Christ, and dying—well, that's better yet! (Philippians 1:20-21)*

RELATED VERSES: *Proverbs 10:24; Luke 8:49-56; Romans 8:38-39; 1 Corinthians 3:22*

RELATED QUESTIONS: *Why is everybody buried together in a cemetery instead of by themselves? How can they make room in the cemetery for everyone who is dead?*

NOTE TO PARENTS: *Help your children develop a healthy attitude about death. Say positive things as you pass a cemetery; don't jokingly say things that foster a fear of death.*

Q: WHY DID GOD TAKE GRANDPA TO HEAVEN?

60

A: We don't like to think about this fact, but it is true—eventually every person has to die. Sometimes people die when they are young, through accidents, diseases, or other tragedies. But even the healthiest person will die someday. As we get older, our bodies get weaker and weaker and then finally wear out.

No one wants a grandfather or grandmother to die, but that's part of God's plan right now: We get old and our bodies die. Certainly it is better to be with God in heaven than to be on earth. If our grandparents believe in Jesus, then someday we will see them again.

KEY VERSE: *[God's] loved ones are very special to him. He does not lightly let them die. (Psalm 116:15)*

RELATED VERSES: *Proverbs 16:31; 20:29*

RELATED QUESTIONS: *When I go up to heaven will I see my grandma? Will God let me visit Grandpa in heaven? If a whole family dies on earth, like in a fire, will they be together in a house in heaven?*

Q: HOW CAN JESUS RESURRECT BODIES THAT HAVE BEEN BURNT TO ASHES?

61

A: God will have no trouble finding everyone's molecules. He created people in the first place, so why wouldn't he be able to put them back together? It doesn't matter what happens to a person's body—God can put anyone back together. Whether the person's body was burned, separated for organ donations, or decayed in the ground, God will make it new and immortal. The earth and sea will give up their dead, and God will resurrect us despite the fact that we "returned to dust."

KEY VERSES: *When Jesus comes back, God will bring back with him all the dead Christians. . . . The believers who are dead will be the first to rise to meet the Lord. Then we who are alive and remain on the earth will be caught up with them. We will go to the clouds to meet the Lord in the air. We will stay with him forever. (1 Thessalonians 4:14, 16-17)*

RELATED VERSES: *Psalm 90:3; Ecclesiastes 3:20; Revelation 20:12-13*

RELATED QUESTIONS: *How can Jesus resurrect your body if it's turned to compost? If people have been dead for a long time, do they turn to compost? If someone hurts you really bad, like a bad person cuts off your head, and God really loves you, will he give you a new body? Isn't it gross to have worms chewing your body after you're dead?*

Q: WHY DO PEOPLE BELIEVE IN REINCARNATION?

62

A: Reincarnation is the belief that people come back to life after they die. They never really die once and for all but keep coming back as something else or as someone else. This belief says that people come back to earth as different creatures after they die.

Some people believe in reincarnation because their religion, such as Hinduism or Buddhism, teaches it. Some believe in reincarnation because they want to believe that they will get a second chance on earth to be better people. But the Bible does not teach reincarnation. The Bible teaches that we have one life and then we face judgment.

KEY VERSE: *It is planned that men die only once. And after that comes judgment. (Hebrews 9:27)*

RELATED VERSES: *Luke 16:19-31*

RELATED QUESTIONS: *Does* born again *mean reincarnation? Is reincarnation replanting carnations? If you die, can you come back as a different person? What does the Bible say about reincarnation?*

NOTE TO PARENTS: *Some children misinterpret the term* born again *to mean reincarnation. You can explain that being born again means to be born into God's family, not to come back as a different person later. Being born again happens when we trust in Jesus Christ as Savior. It's not reincarnation.*

Q: WHAT'S A CASKET?

63

A: A casket is a metal or wooden box in which a dead body is placed. Usually a casket is buried in the ground in a cemetery. Putting a body in a casket is a very old custom and is a way of showing respect for the dead person. Also, it is part of the custom of mourning the person's death.

KEY VERSE: *It will be an honor to have you [Abraham] choose the finest of our tombs, so that you can bury [Sarah] there. (Genesis 23:6)*

RELATED VERSES: *Genesis 50:26; Amos 2:1; Mark 15:46; Romans 12:15*

RELATED QUESTIONS: *How can people be cremated? How can adults be cremated when they're so big?*

Q: WHY DO PEOPLE CRY AT FUNERALS?

64

A: People cry at funerals because they are very sad. They miss the person who has died. Even when people know that their family member or friend is now in heaven with Jesus, they cry because they miss their loved one. The purpose of funerals is to say good-bye to the dead person, to show respect for the person and his or her family, to cry and be sad, and to remember what the person meant to everyone.

KEY VERSES: *Tears came to Jesus' eyes. "They were close friends," the Jewish leaders said. "See how much he loved him." (John 11:35-36)*

RELATED VERSES: *Mark 5:38-39; Luke 7:11-15; Romans 12:15*

RELATED QUESTION: *Why do we have funerals?*

Q: WHY DO THEY PUT STONES ON PEOPLE'S GRAVES?

Rock vs. Paper →

R.I.P.

R.I.P.

65

A: A gravestone or metal plate on a grave marks the place where the person's body is buried. After a person has died, friends and family will sometimes go to the cemetery, put flowers on the grave, and think about that person. The stone helps them find the grave. They can go there and remember the person instead of forgetting. Just think what it would be like if a family member was buried and no one marked where the grave was.

KEY VERSE: *The Lord buried [Moses] in a valley near Beth-peor in Moab. But no one knows the exact place. (Deuteronomy 34:6)*

RELATED VERSE: *Acts 13:36*

RELATED QUESTIONS: *Why do people talk to dead people at their graves? Why do people visit people's graves if their spirits have already gone to heaven?*

Q: WHY DO WE GIVE FLOWERS TO PEOPLE AFTER THEY HAVE DIED?

66

A: Many people bring flowers to funerals, wakes, and gravesides. It looks as though they are giving something to someone who can't enjoy the gift. Why would they do that? It is to show respect and to show that they miss the person. It's like saying, "I wish you were still here. I love you. I miss you." Also, flowers remind us of life. Most important, people give flowers to honor the person and the family of the person who has died. Flowers on a casket or on a grave say, "This person was important to me."

KEY VERSE: *When others are happy, be happy with them. If they are sad, share their sadness. (Romans 12:15)*

RELATED VERSES: *Isaiah 40:6; Amos 2:1; 1 Peter 1:24; 2:17*

LIVING
IN
HEAVEN

Q: WILL I BE ABLE TO PLAY GAMES IN HEAVEN?

67

A: Heaven will be more exciting than you could possibly imagine. Will that mean playing lots of games? Probably not—you can get bored with games, and life in heaven will *never* be boring. You will never get tired of what you're doing there. The Bible says that you will always be happy in heaven. If you think games are fun, you should see what's coming next—it will be *much* better than playing games all the time.

It's OK if you don't understand this. Trying to understand life in heaven is like trying to understand how fun an amusement park will be before you get there. How can you really know what to expect? You can't. All you can do is hear the descriptions ("It's great! It's wonderful! You can ride on the SuperCollosalMachine!"). Until you go, you won't *really* be able to get excited about it. But once you're there, *wow!*

KEY VERSE: *We can see and understand only a little about God now. It is like we were looking at his reflection in a poor mirror. Someday we are going to see him face to face. Now all that I know is hazy and blurred. But then I will see everything clearly. (1 Corinthians 13:12)*

RELATED VERSES: *1 Corinthians 13:11-12; Revelation 4:8-11; 7:15-17; 22:3*

RELATED QUESTIONS: *Will there be lots and lots of toys in heaven? Will I still get to drive a car when I'm in heaven, or can you take a bus somewhere?*

NOTE TO PARENTS: *The tadpole analogy (see the next question) is useful for questions about boredom in heaven.*

Q: IN HEAVEN, WE DON'T JUST SING AND WORSHIP ALL DAY, DO WE?

68

A: In heaven, we will be happy all the time. Heaven will be a place made just for us. We read in the Bible about angels singing and praising God day and night, and we can't imagine doing that all the time. But remember that they are singing because they are *glad*. They aren't bored, tired, or old. They are expressing happiness and joy. God is the happiest person in the universe, and living in heaven means being there with him doing the same thing. Life with God is happy, joyful, and cool.

Imagine that you're a tadpole. All your life you've lived only in the water. You know that someday you'll become a frog and you'll get to live on land. But until you become a frog, you will have no idea what life on land is like. And if anyone tries to explain it to you, it won't sound very appealing because there's no water and you can't swim. That's the way it is with heaven. Until we get to heaven, it will be hard for us to understand what's so great about it. But once we're there, we'll be perfect and we'll have new bodies, and that will make all the difference.

KEY VERSE: *Now I can sing glad praises to the Lord. I can sing instead of lying in silence in the grave. (Psalm 30:12)*

RELATED VERSES: *Psalm 61:8; 89:1; Isaiah 35:10; 51:11; 1 Corinthians 2:9; 13:12; Revelation 4:8-11; 7:15-17*

RELATED QUESTIONS: *Won't heaven be boring? Will I be bored in heaven?*

NOTE TO PARENTS: *Children can understand singing for joy by thinking of songs they sing when they're happy or celebrating. What they feel when singing those songs is like what they will feel in heaven—only better!*

Q: WHAT WILL I DO UP THERE WITH NO FRIENDS?

69

A: If your friends believe in Jesus, they will be in heaven with you, and you will have a *great* time together. Jesus is preparing a place for us; he won't keep us apart from each other. And we'll make new friends in heaven, too. If you aren't sure whether your friends will go to heaven, tell them about Jesus. If they put their faith in Christ, too, you will all be there together.

You don't have to worry—heaven *won't* be boring. Remember, God created butterflies, sunsets, electrical storms, mountains, the Grand Canyon, and all of nature. He will give us so much fun, beauty, and joy in heaven that we can hardly imagine it now.

KEY VERSES: *There are many homes in my Father's house. I am going to prepare a place for you. I will come again and take you to me. Then you will be with me where I am about to go. (John 14:2-3)*

RELATED VERSES: *1 Thessalonians 4:13-17*

RELATED QUESTIONS: *Who can I play with when I die? Will I be able to play with my friends up in heaven? Will I remember my family and friends in heaven? Will there be any stuffed animals? Is there going to be any paint in God's world? What happens when we go to heaven?*

Q: WILL I STILL HAVE FEELINGS IN HEAVEN?

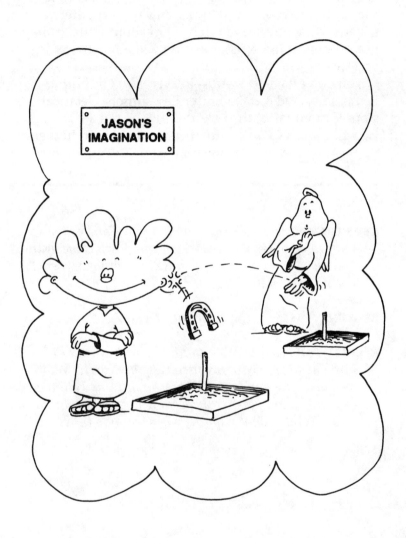

70

A: Yes! People in heaven have lots of feelings—all good ones. People in heaven are filled with joy! You will be busy smiling, whistling, and singing for joy. When you are not doing that, you will be kicking your heels and jumping. Occasional high fives will interrupt the joviality. The timing will be perfect, and you'll love it. You will be happy because you will be with God and because all sin, death, and sadness will be gone forever. And think of the joy when you see your family and friends. Heaven will be a place of great joy and gladness—great feelings all around.

KEY VERSE: *You will give me back my life. You will give me great joy in your presence. (Acts 2:28)*

RELATED VERSES: *Jeremiah 31:13; Matthew 25:34; John 16:20-22*

Q: CAN WE STILL HAVE BIRTHDAYS IN HEAVEN?

71

A: The great thing about birthdays is the parties. In heaven, we won't grow old, but we will have lots of parties. The biggest party will be the celebration of "the wedding feast of the Lamb," when we celebrate our new life in heaven with Jesus. It will be ten times more fun than any birthday you've ever had.

The things we enjoy here on earth are like appetizers. They give us only a taste of what heaven will be like. The things you enjoy here on earth will only be better and greater in the presence of God.

KEY VERSE: *And the angel spoke to me. He said, "Blessed are those who are invited to the wedding feast of the Lamb." (Revelation 19:9)*

RELATED VERSES: *Isaiah 25:6-8*

NOTE TO PARENTS: *Heaven lacks a lot of the things that kids enjoy—toys, television, and games. This confuses many kids because they think they need these things to be happy. They don't realize that enjoyment of kid things depends on their being kids. In heaven they won't be kids anymore—they'll be perfect, so they'll enjoy different things. What will make us happy in heaven will match who we will be then, and that's something we can't see very well right now (1 Corinthians 13:12).*

Q: WILL YOU SEE YOUR GREAT-GREAT-GRANDPARENTS IN HEAVEN?

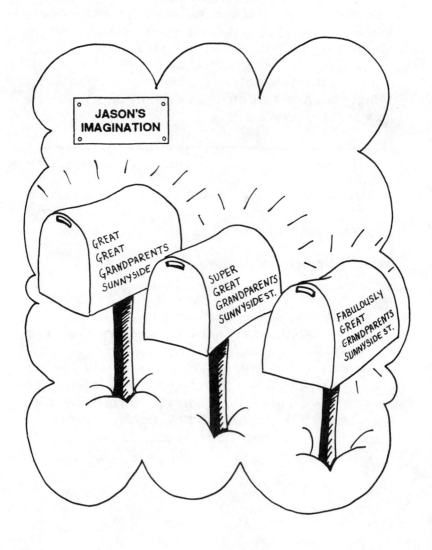

72

A: All people who have ever believed in Jesus, no matter how long ago, will be in heaven. If your great-great-grandparents believed in Jesus, they will be there. Even though you have never met your great-great-grandparents, you will be able to meet them there. But not every person who ever lived has believed, so not every person will be there.

KEY VERSE: *God has reserved for his children the priceless gift of eternal life. It is kept in Heaven for you. It is pure and spotless. It is beyond the reach of change and decay. (1 Peter 1:4)*

RELATED VERSES: *Romans 16:26; Hebrews 12:22-24; 1 Peter 1:3-5; 2 Peter 1:11; Revelation 7:9*

NOTE TO PARENTS: *This kind of question could mean, "In heaven, will we see all people who have ever lived?" The answer is, "No, only those who have trusted in Christ as Savior." Or it could mean that your child is curious about past relatives whom he or she has never met. If great-great-grandparents and others were believers, this would be a great time to tell about your family's heritage of faith.*

Q: WILL WE LOOK LIKE WE DO NOW IN HEAVEN?

73

A: No one knows *exactly* what we will look like in heaven, but the Bible makes it clear that we will have new bodies—resurrected and perfect bodies. We will be different, but we surely won't be strangers to each other. We will be able to recognize each other and enjoy each other's company, just as we do here on earth—except it will be better because we'll never fight!

KEY VERSE: *When [Christ] comes back, he will change these dying bodies of ours. He will make them into glorious bodies like his own. (Philippians 3:21)*

RELATED VERSES: *Matthew 17:1-13; Luke 16:19-31; 1 Corinthians 15:35-58*

RELATED QUESTIONS: *Do you look like yourself in heaven? When people are dead, why don't they look like themselves? What will we look like in heaven?*

Q: WHEN WE GO TO HEAVEN, WILL WE GET SNARLS IN OUR HAIR?

74

A: Nope. Heaven is a place of happiness and joy—a place of no pain. We won't have irritations and frustrations. Also, we'll have new, "glorified" bodies. Our hair won't be the kind that snarls.

KEY VERSE: *Every human being has a body just like Adam's, made of dust. But all who become Christ's will have the same kind of body as his. It is a body from Heaven. (1 Corinthians 15:48)*

RELATED VERSES: *1 Corinthians 15:35-58; Revelation 21:4*

RELATED QUESTIONS: *If you just ask for something in heaven, will it just appear before you? Will there be any schools in heaven?*

Q: WILL PEOPLE HAVE SCARS IN HEAVEN?

75

A: In heaven, everyone will have new bodies, and no one will feel any pain. There will be no physical or mental disabilities. Everybody will be able to sing, think, talk, run, and play . . . without growing tired. People may have scars, but they won't look bad.

KEY VERSE: *The bodies we have now shame us. They become sick and die. But they will be full of glory when we come back to life again. Yes, they are weak, dying bodies now. But when we live again they will be strong. (1 Corinthians 15:43)*

RELATED VERSES: *Luke 24:40; John 20:27; 1 Corinthians 15:35-53; 2 Corinthians 4:16–5:5; Revelation 21:4*

NOTE TO PARENTS: *The pattern for heaven should be our pattern, too: to affirm people as they are, not reject them for being different or "imperfect."*

Q: ARE THERE ANIMALS IN HEAVEN?

76

A: When God creates the new heaven and the new earth, he will make all of creation new, and that includes the animal kingdom. But keep in mind that the animals won't be just like they are here on earth. They won't be dangerous. They won't attack people or be afraid of us. And all of them will get along with each other; they won't need to eat other animals. The Bible also says there will be plant life in heaven, such as trees. And perhaps best of all, no one will be allergic to any of it—dogs, cats, pollen, or anything!

KEY VERSE: *In that day the wolf and the lamb will lie down together. And the leopard and goats will be at peace. (Isaiah 11:6)*

RELATED VERSES: *Isaiah 11:6-9; 55:12-13; Romans 8:18-21; Revelation 22:2*

RELATED QUESTIONS: *If God made everything, will there be dragons in heaven? Will only dogs go to heaven? Will insects go to heaven? Will there be any lizards in heaven? Will there be any birds in the new world? Will my pet go to heaven when it dies? Will there be any feathers and ducks in heaven? Will there be any reindeers in heaven? Are there going to be any mice or frogs?*

NOTE TO PARENTS: *There is no evidence in the Bible that animals will be resurrected. So we don't really know if a child's pet will be in heaven with him or her. All we know is that we will have in heaven whatever we need to be happy.*

Q: WILL WE EAT IN HEAVEN?

77

A: We will be *able* to eat in heaven, but we won't *have* to eat to live, as we do on earth. Jesus said he would eat with his people there. But no one in heaven will ever go hungry.

KEY VERSE: *Here in Jerusalem the Lord Almighty will spread a great feast. It will be for everyone around the world. It will be a tasty feast of good food. There will be clear, well-aged wine and choice beef. (Isaiah 25:6)*

RELATED VERSE: *Matthew 26:29*

RELATED QUESTIONS: *Does heaven have hotels or inns? What do angels eat? Are angels fat? Is there junk food up in heaven? What does Jesus eat in heaven? Will there be restaurants to eat at in heaven? Are there food fights in heaven? Does heaven have sections for candy, one for cereal, etc.? Will they have Kool-Aid in heaven?*

Q: WILL WE WEAR CLOTHES IN HEAVEN?

78

A: The Bible says that people will wear clothes in heaven—dazzling white robes. But people won't wear clothes for the same reasons that they wear them here. On earth, people wear clothes to protect them from bad weather, to cover their nakedness, and to impress other people. We won't need clothes to protect us from the cold because it won't be cold. We won't need raincoats because it won't be stormy. And we won't need special designer clothes because we won't need to show off.

KEY VERSE: *I saw a great crowd, too big to count. They were from all nations and lands and languages. I saw them standing in front of the throne and before the Lamb. They were dressed in white. And they had palm branches in their hands. (Revelation 7:9)*

RELATED VERSES: *Mark 9:3; Revelation 3:18; 4:4*

RELATED QUESTIONS: *Will people be naked in heaven? Do angels have to buy things? Why are some angels naked?*

Q: DO BABIES STAY IN HEAVEN UNTIL THEY ARE BORN?

79

A: Whenever God creates a person, he creates a new soul, a new person who never existed before. Babies do not live in heaven waiting to be born here on earth. The starting place for every person is right inside the mother's womb.

KEY VERSE: *You made all the parts of my body. You put them together in my mother's womb. (Psalm 139:13)*

RELATED VERSES: *Genesis 1:27-28; 2:7; 1 Corinthians 11:8*

Q: DO PEOPLE WALK IN HEAVEN, OR DO THEY FLY TO WHERE THEY NEED TO BE?

80

A: We don't know for sure how people get around in heaven. The Bible does say that angels fly, but it never says that people have wings or that they fly around, not even in heaven. Usually descriptions of people in heaven talk about them standing or walking.

KEY VERSE: *I saw a great crowd, too big to count. They were from all nations and lands and languages. I saw them standing in front of the throne and before the Lamb. They were dressed in white. And they had palm branches in their hands. (Revelation 7:9)*

RELATED VERSE: *Revelation 14:6*

Q: DOES JESUS COME INTO YOUR HOUSE IN HEAVEN FOR A VISIT?

81

A: Jesus always visits those who let him in. On earth, Jesus often visited his friends Mary, Martha, and Lazarus. In his early ministry, he went to a friend's wedding. And just before Jesus went to the cross, he told his disciples that he would eat and drink with them in heaven. Jesus will visit all of his friends in heaven, including you. Just think—we will finally get to see him face-to-face!

KEY VERSE: *Mark my [Jesus'] words. I will not drink wine again until I drink it with you in my Father's Kingdom. (Matthew 26:29)*

RELATED VERSES: *Mark 14:25; Luke 22:18; John 12:1-3; 14:2; 21:4-14; Revelation 3:20*

RELATED QUESTIONS: *Can you have a sleepover with God when you're in heaven? Will there be a lot of windows in our house? Will we be able to walk through walls when we're in heaven? Do they have furniture in heaven?*

NOTE TO PARENTS: *Above all else, God seeks a relationship with us. That is why he created us, that is why he sent his Son to die for us, and that is why he is preparing a place for us. Remind your child that being with us matters very much to God—now, as well as in heaven.*

Q: WHAT WOULD HAPPEN IF I ACCIDENTALLY SWORE IN HEAVEN?

82

A: You will *never* accidentally swear in heaven, because no one in heaven can sin. You cannot do wrong in God's presence. Jesus will make all of his people perfect, like himself, so you won't *want* to sin. Messing up is one thing you'll never have to worry about again.

KEY VERSE: *Yes, dear friends, we are already God's children. We can't imagine what it is going to be like later on. But we do know that when he comes we will be like him. We shall see him as he really is. (1 John 3:2)*

RELATED VERSE: *1 Corinthians 13:12*

RELATED QUESTIONS: *Is heaven as nice as we think? If I swear, will I go to hell when I die?*

NOTE TO PARENTS: *The real concern here may be that your children do not feel they are good enough to get into heaven. Assure them that if they believe in Jesus as their Savior, they will go to heaven. Also, as they pray and trust God to help them, they will become more like Jesus.*

Q: DO YOU PRAY IN HEAVEN OR JUST TALK TO GOD FACE-TO-FACE?

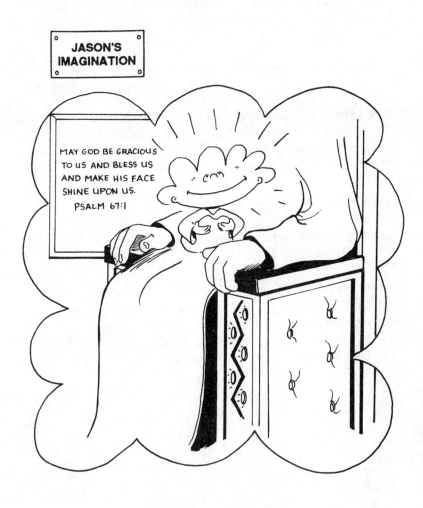

83

A:

We will be able to talk to God face-to-face. (Moses talked with God face-to-face on earth, but that was unusual.) Remember, God wants to be our friend. Right now we are separated a little, and we have to pray to talk to God. But that relationship will be made perfect in heaven. Finally we will be able to go right up to God and talk to him, just as we have always wanted to do. In heaven, we will see God just as he is.

KEY VERSE: *We can see and understand only a little about God now. It is like we were looking at his reflection in a poor mirror. Someday we are going to see him face to face. Now all that I know is hazy and blurred. But then I will see everything clearly. I will see as clearly as God sees into my heart right now. (1 Corinthians 13:12)*

RELATED VERSES: *Exodus 33:11; Acts 7:56-59; 1 Thessalonians 5:10; Revelation 4:8-11; 21:3-4*

RELATED QUESTIONS: *Will we be able to see God when we are in heaven? Will I get to see and be with Jesus in heaven? When you're visiting with Jesus in heaven, does he know what you're going to say before you say it?*

Q: WILL WE LIVE WITH ANGELS IN HEAVEN?

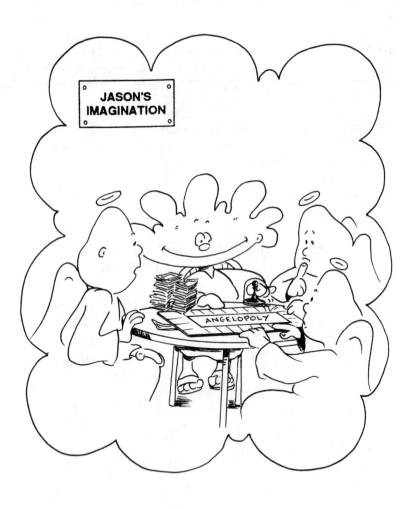

84

A: We will live with God and the angels. But the angels will not be equal to us there. The angels are God's messengers, his servants. Part of the angels' job is to help us here on earth. Our friends and family in heaven will be the people we have known here on earth and other Christians who have died. Remember, angels aren't people; they're God's servants.

KEY VERSE: *Don't you know that we will judge the angels in Heaven? (1 Corinthians 6:3)*

RELATED VERSES: *John 14:3; Hebrews 1:14*

RELATED QUESTION: *Who will live with angels in heaven?*

Q: WILL THERE BE ANY CHURCH IN HEAVEN?

85

A: There will be no churches or temples in heaven because we won't need them. We will be right there in the presence of God. We will be perfect and sinless, so we won't need to go to Sunday school to learn about God or about how to obey him. We won't need worship leaders because we will worship just by being there. We will know God and see him face-to-face.

KEY VERSE: *No temple could be seen in the city. Why? Because the Lord God Almighty and the Lamb are worshiped in it everywhere. (Revelation 21:22)*

RELATED VERSES: *1 Corinthians 13:12; Revelation 21:1–22:17*

NOTE TO PARENTS: *After a question like this, explain the purpose of the church on earth and why it is necessary to attend. Also, if your child views church as boring, he may be asking if heaven is boring. Assure him that heaven is a wonderful, exciting place.*

Q: WILL GOD BE WITH ME ALL THE TIME IN HEAVEN?

86

A: Yes! In heaven, you will get to go right up to God and talk to him. God will be with you all the time, and you will be with him. God will be your friend, and you will be his. Getting to be with God will be one of heaven's greatest joys.

KEY VERSE: *I heard a loud shout from the throne. It was saying, "Look, the home of God is now among men. He will live with them and they will be his people. Yes, God himself will be among them." (Revelation 21:3)*

RELATED VERSES: *1 Corinthians 13:12; 2 Corinthians 5:8*

RELATED QUESTION: *Can God be my best friend?*

Q: WILL THERE BE A BIBLE "HALL OF FAME" IN HEAVEN?

87

A: Some people think that heaven is just like earth, with shopping malls, schools, athletic stadiums, and airports. But heaven is very different from earth. The focus in heaven is on God, not people. We will praise and worship God because no one's fame can compare with his.

People *will* be honored in heaven, however. The Bible says that believers will receive rewards for their good deeds. The greatest reward, of course, is just getting there. God gives salvation—a free gift made possible by Jesus' death on the cross—to all who put their faith in Christ. He will give other rewards to every believer who does good deeds for God on earth. Everyone's service will be rewarded.

KEY VERSE: *See, I am coming soon, and my reward is with me. I will repay everyone according to the deeds he has done. (Revelation 22:12)*

RELATED VERSES: *Romans 5:1; 14:12; 1 Corinthians 3:9-15; 9:16-27; 2 Corinthians 5:10; Revelation 3:5*

RELATED QUESTIONS: *Does God give out awards in heaven? Will there be a president in heaven?*

NOTE TO PARENTS: *It's easy to confuse rewards for good service with salvation by works. We receive our salvation by faith, not good deeds!*

Q: CAN WE SEE PEOPLE FROM THE BIBLE IN HEAVEN?

88

A: Everyone who has ever trusted in Christ for salvation will be in heaven, and that includes all the Bible people who ever believed. You will get to know them, too. They can be your new friends!

KEY VERSE: *God wanted them [his people in the Bible] to wait and share the better rewards that were prepared for us. (Hebrews 11:40)*

RELATED VERSES: *2 Samuel 12:22-23; Matthew 17:3; Luke 23:43; Hebrews 12:1*

NOTE TO PARENTS: *When reading Bible stories, remind your children that the stories are true and that the Bible heroes are living now with God. This should help to make the stories more real.*

Q: WHY CAN'T I SEE JESUS NOW?

89

A: Jesus went back to heaven to be with his Father, but he has *not* forgotten about his people. In fact, he is preparing a place for all who believe in him, getting it ready for when they die and go to be with him. Also, Jesus is acting as our High Priest (like in the Old Testament)—whenever his people sin, he presents his own death as a payment so God can forgive them.

You may remember that the Bible calls Satan the Accuser. That's because he tells God the believers' faults to get God to reject his people. (There's an example in Job 1:6-11.) Whenever the devil accuses a believer, Jesus defends that person. We can't see Jesus now because it's not a part of God's plan.

Meanwhile, Jesus has not left his people alone. He has sent the Holy Spirit to be with them wherever they go. That's why Jesus said, "It is best for you that I go away" (John 16:7). When Jesus comes back, he will take all believers to live with him forever. Then you *will* be able to see Jesus in person.

KEY VERSE: *It is best for you that I [Jesus] go away. For if I don't, the Comforter won't come. If I do, he will. For I will send him to you. (John 16:7)*

RELATED VERSES: *Job 1:6-11; John 14:2-20, 28; Acts 1:9-11; 1 Corinthians 13:12*

RELATED QUESTIONS: *Why did God stop sending angels to people in visions? How come God had to use angels? Why do angels come to you and not God himself?*

THE
END
OF THE
WORLD

Q: WHEN WILL THE WORLD END?

JASON'S PRAYER

Lord, please
come quickly
To end all sin
and hurt.
But if you're
coming today
PLEASE, after
dessert.

90

A: The world will not end until God is ready to take all believers home to heaven. It will happen when God decides that it is the right time. And no one knows when that time will come. Only God the Father knows. People who trust in God should not be afraid about the world coming to an end because it will be God's time of rescuing them from trouble and pain.

KEY VERSES: *Heaven and earth shall disappear. But my words stand sure forever. However, no one knows the day or hour when these things will happen. The angels in Heaven don't even know. I myself don't know. Only the Father knows. (Mark 13:31-32)*

RELATED VERSES: *Matthew 10:22; John 16:33; 2 Peter 3:10; Revelation 7:14-17*

RELATED QUESTION: *When is the world finished?*

Q: HOW WILL THE WORLD END?

91

A: The world will not end by an accident but by God's power. Right now God keeps the world safe from being destroyed. But someday, at the time he decides, God will burn up the world with fire. Then he will create a new heaven and a new earth, where all believers will live forever.

KEY VERSE: *The day of the Lord is surely coming. It will come as suddenly as a thief in the night. Then the heavens will pass away with a terrible noise. The heavenly bodies will disappear in fire [after we are gone]. The earth and everything on it will be burned up. (2 Peter 3:10)*

RELATED VERSES: *Mark 13:7; 2 Peter 3:10-14*

RELATED QUESTION: *Will God burn up the world?*

Q: IF JESUS HAS ALREADY WON, WHY IS EVERYONE STILL FIGHTING?

92

A: Jesus won over sin and death when he rose from the dead. But some people still sin and fight because they don't love or follow Jesus. Jesus is waiting for them to change their minds and follow him. As Jesus waits, they do what their sinful desires tell them to—they sin and fight. Satan has not surrendered, and he still tries to trick people. Jesus hasn't come back yet because he loves us all and wants many more people to trust in him as Savior so they can be saved from hell and go to heaven.

Jesus has won over sin and death, but he won't *make* us live at peace with each other. The more we love him, the more we learn to live at peace and not fight.

KEY VERSE: *When you understand you are useless before the Lord, he will lift you up. He will encourage and help you. (James 4:10)*

RELATED VERSES: *James 3:16; 4:1-6; 2 Peter 3:9-15*

RELATED QUESTION: *Why hasn't Jesus come back yet?*

Q: WHAT HAPPENS TO THE BAD PEOPLE WHEN JESUS COMES BACK?

93

A:
When Jesus comes back to earth, people who know Jesus will be glad. But people who don't know Jesus will be very sad and afraid because they will be judged for their sin. Those who have not believed in Jesus as their Savior will be punished and sent to hell, far away from God. That is one of the reasons God urges us to tell our friends about Jesus—so they can join us and God in heaven.

KEY VERSE: *[Nonbelievers] will be punished in everlasting hell. They will be forever separated from the Lord. They will never see the glory of his power. (2 Thessalonians 1:9)*

RELATED VERSES: *1 Corinthians 4:5; 2 Thessalonians 1:6-10; 2 Timothy 4:1; Jude 1:14-15; Revelation 20:11-15*

RELATED QUESTIONS: *Will everyone see Jesus when he comes back? Does God ever fight back? Does God fight everyone that is or was bad? Will the bad people be crushed when the new Jerusalem lands on them?*

NOTE TO PARENTS: *Be careful not to divide the world between "good people" and "bad people." Many so-called good people don't trust in Christ, and they will be judged for their sin. Meanwhile, some Christians do bad things, yet they will receive eternal life because of their faith in Christ.*

Q: HOW CAN GOD MOVE A WHOLE CITY DOWN TO EARTH?

94

A: The apostle John had a vision of God bringing the new Jerusalem, the Holy City, down from heaven. We don't know exactly how this will work, but it will happen—God can do anything. He created all the stars and planets, as well as all the plants, animals, and human beings. He can certainly create a new city and bring it to earth.

KEY VERSE: *And I, John, saw the Holy City, the new Jerusalem. It was coming down from God out of Heaven. (Revelation 21:2)*

RELATED VERSE: *Revelation 3:12*

RELATED QUESTION: *What's going to happen to the houses and buildings on earth when the new Jerusalem comes?*

Q: WHEN JESUS COMES TO GET US, WHAT WILL HAPPEN TO EARTH AND EVERYONE ELSE?

95

A: When Jesus comes back to rescue all who believe in him, several things will happen: (1) Jesus will bring life on earth to an end. (2) Jesus will judge everyone. (3) Jesus will create a new heaven and new earth. (4) We will begin eternal life with God. (5) The devil, his demons, and all unbelievers will begin their eternal death in hell.

KEY VERSE: *Then I saw a new earth and a new Heaven. The first earth and Heaven had disappeared. And there was no more sea. (Revelation 21:1)*

RELATED VERSES: *1 Thessalonians 4:16-17; 2 Peter 3:10; Revelation 21:1–22:21*

RELATED QUESTIONS: *In the new Jerusalem will I be Jewish? Will God still be making things in heaven? Who's the archangel who blows the trumpet? Jesus said he wouldn't destroy the earth by rain anymore, but could he destroy it by fire?*

Q: WHEN WILL JESUS COME BACK?

96

A: No one knows when Jesus will come back, not even the angels. God has chosen not to tell us. God has also warned us not to listen to people who say they know when Jesus will return. The day of Christ's return will come "like a thief in the night," when no one is expecting it. People who say they know the date of Christ's return are just trying to trick you. You don't have to worry about missing Jesus when he returns. When Jesus comes back, it will be obvious to everyone. All people all over the world will know.

KEY VERSE: *No one knows the date and hour when the end will be. Not even the angels know this. No, not even God's Son knows this. Only the Father knows. (Matthew 24:36)*

RELATED VERSES: *Matthew 24:23-24, 36-44; Luke 21:8-9; 1 Thessalonians 5:1-11; 2 Thessalonians 2:1-6; 1 Peter 4:7*

RELATED QUESTIONS: *When will the world see God? Will Jesus be able to see everyone at once when he comes back? Does Jesus know when he's coming back? Will everyone see Jesus when he comes back? How could we see Jesus if he comes back on the other side of the earth? Will we hear something when Jesus comes back so we'll know to look up in the sky?*

MISTER
AND
MISCELLANEOUS

Q: WOULD GOD MAKE A FRIENDLY GHOST LIKE CASPER?

97

A: No. Some people in the Bible thought they saw a ghost (a spirit) at times. When the disciples saw Jesus walking on the water, they thought he was a ghost. When an angel freed Peter from prison and his friend Rhoda saw him, she thought she was seeing "his angel." When Jesus appeared to his disciples after he rose from the dead, he said he was not a ghost. And some Bible translations use the word *ghost* to mean "spirit." But the Bible does *not* teach that spirits fly around visiting people. Many people have believed that after death, people come back as ghosts. But that's not taught in the Bible at all.

Some people call the Holy Spirit the Holy Ghost. When Jesus left the earth, he sent the Holy Spirit to live within us. He is the one who comforts, guides, and protects us.

KEY VERSE: *Then the Father will send the Comforter to you. The Comforter is the Holy Spirit. He will teach you much. And he will remind you of everything I myself have told you. (John 14:26)*

RELATED VERSES: *Matthew 14:26; Luke 24:39; John 14:15-26; Acts 12:1-19*

RELATED QUESTIONS: *Did God make ghosts? Can people come back from heaven to visit earth?*

Q: WHY DO SOME PEOPLE BELIEVE IN GHOSTS?

98

A: A ghost is a disembodied spirit—the spirit of a person separated from the body. Some people believe in ghosts because they have heard about them on television shows, in movies, and in cartoons, and because many other people believe in ghosts. Some people believe in them because they have had strange experiences that they can't explain, and they figure that ghosts are the only answer.

The Bible gives no evidence that people come back to earth without their bodies. When you die, God takes your spirit from earth forever—believers into God's presence, unbelievers to a place of suffering. People do not come back as ghosts.

KEY VERSE: *It is planned that men die only once. And after that comes judgment. (Hebrews 9:27)*

RELATED VERSES: *Matthew 14:26-27; Luke 16:19-31; 24:37-39*

RELATED QUESTIONS: *When you are dead and you're up in heaven, could you talk to somebody on earth still? How can people come back from heaven when the doctors bring them back to life? If someone has a heart attack and dies and goes to heaven for a couple seconds and then comes back again, is it because the doctor saves him? Can people come back from heaven to visit earth?*

Q: WHY DID SAUL GO TO A FORTUNE-TELLER?

99

A: King Saul went to see a medium, or fortune-teller, because he was desperate. He did not trust in God to lead him. Saul wanted to find out things that he didn't have a right to know. In the law, God had told his people that they should never get involved with witchcraft, mediums, and fortune-tellers. Saul disobeyed God and did it anyway.

KEY VERSE: *Saul then ordered his aides to try to find a medium. He wanted to ask her what to do. (1 Samuel 28:7)*

RELATED VERSES: *Deuteronomy 18:10-11; 1 Samuel 28:3-25; Acts 16:16*

RELATED QUESTIONS: *How can people see things in crystal balls? Does celebrating Halloween make God unhappy? Is a séance when a dead person talks at their own funeral?*

NOTE TO PARENTS: *Dabbling in the occult is not a harmless pastime. Satan and demons are real beings that can influence the physical world, and occult practices only invite them to do so. Don't have Ouija boards, tarot cards, or other forms of occult fortune-telling in your home, and don't let your kids use them either. Remind your child that God loves us, has good plans for us, and has given us the Holy Spirit. He will give us wisdom if we ask him (James 1:5).*

Q: WHY DO SOME PEOPLE BELIEVE THAT TREES, PLANTS, AND ANIMALS HAVE SPIRITS?

100

A: Some people believe that trees, plants, and animals have spirits because they are confused. Plants and animals don't have spirits, but many false religions teach that they do. Only *people* have eternal souls.

At the same time, God does want us to respect the world he created. God created all living things, including plants and animals. The Bible says that all of nature groans under the weight of our sin. And some of the psalms in the Bible say, as a figure of speech, that the trees of the fields will clap their hands in praise of God. But plants and animals don't have spirits. And even more important to remember is that we are to worship only God, not anyone or anything else.

KEY VERSE: *Praise [God] for the growing fields. For they prove his greatness. Let the trees of the forest rustle with praise. (Psalm 96:12)*

RELATED VERSES: *Exodus 20:3-5; Isaiah 1:29; 55:12; 57:5-6; Hosea 4:13*

RELATED QUESTIONS: *When my pet dies, does it go to heaven or hell? Is the New Age movement when people move to a new place? What is the New Age movement?*

Q: WHY DO THEY PUT HOROSCOPES IN THE NEWSPAPER?

101

A: Newspapers print horoscopes because many people want to read them. And people read horoscopes because they believe that major parts of life are controlled by outside forces beyond their control. They look to the horoscopes for guidance.

Believers should not look to horoscopes for guidance. Only God controls what happens, and only God knows the future. If we need advice, we should do three things: (1) read the Bible, (2) talk to wise people (Proverbs 13:20), and (3) ask God for wisdom (James 1:5). If you are worried about the future, the best thing to do is to pray and tell God about your worries, ask him to take care of you, and trust him to do it (Philippians 4:6).

KEY VERSE: *[God's people] must not be serpent charmers, mediums, or wizards. They must never call forth the spirits of the dead. (Deuteronomy 18:11)*

RELATED VERSES: *Deuteronomy 18:10-13; 2 Kings 17:16-17; Psalm 147:4; Isaiah 34:4; Philippians 4:6; James 1:5; 1 Peter 5:7*

RELATED QUESTIONS: *Why do some people try to trick other people by saying they can tell fortunes? Is ESP some kind of tax?*

NOTE TO PARENTS: *Horoscopes are closely related to occult practices. It's better to turn to God for guidance, wisdom, and assurance for the future.*

Q: WHY ARE THERE SPOOKY THINGS LIKE SKELETONS AND MONSTERS?

102

A: Some people like to be frightened by funny skeletons and make-believe monsters. And they like scaring others, especially at Halloween. But you don't have to be afraid of ghosts and goblins because they aren't real. Besides, God is with you and will take care of you. Keep trusting in him to protect you.

KEY VERSE: *Be strong! Be brave! Do not be afraid of them! For the Lord your God will be with you. He will neither fail you nor forsake you. (Deuteronomy 31:6)*

RELATED VERSES: *Matthew 28:20; Luke 12:4-5; John 16:33*

RELATED QUESTIONS: *Are there such things as haunted houses? Are ghosts real? If ghosts are real, are they the devil's demons? Why are there monsters? Why is there Halloween?*

Q: ARE ANGELS OUR IMAGINARY FRIENDS?

103

A: Angels are real, not imaginary. Some people think they can talk to angels or that they have special angels who guide them. But the Bible teaches that angels are God's messengers—they serve him and do what he says. Often God tells them to help us. But they're not our friends the way people are or even the way God can be. Angels are God's servants, not people's, but they are as real as God is.

KEY VERSE: *For the Lord saves those who respect him. The Angel of the Lord guards them. (Psalm 34:7)*

RELATED VERSE: *Hebrews 1:14*

RELATED QUESTION: *Can angels tell people about Jesus?*

NOTE TO PARENTS: *A lot of children go through stages when they have imaginary friends, and many children may believe these friends are angels. This can be an ideal time to introduce them to a Friend who will always be with them—Jesus.*

Q: IF I DIE WHEN I'M A KID, WILL I MISS OUT ON DOING FUN THINGS ON EARTH?

104

A: When people die, their life on earth ends. That's true no matter how young or old a person is when he or she dies. But do these people miss their "fun" on earth? Are they up in heaven being sad about all the fun things they didn't get to do? Not at all! Living in the presence of God is the most enjoyable thing a person can do. It is what we were created for.

Don't worry—God has a wonderful plan for your life here on earth. Enjoy the life God has given you. You won't be sorry you went to heaven when the time comes for you to go!

KEY VERSES: *Sometimes I want to live, and at other times I don't. For I long to go and be with Christ. How much happier for me than being here! But I can be of more help to you by staying! (Philippians 1:23-24)*

RELATED VERSES: *Mark 12:25; Philippians 1:21-24*

RELATED QUESTIONS: *Will there be candy and television in heaven? Do they have video games in heaven? Do I get to stay up and not go to bed in heaven? Will there be Legos in heaven? If you die when you're a kid and go to heaven, can you get married? Will there be cartoons in heaven?*